W9-APF-586

The Tragedy of Patton

A Soldier's Date with Destiny

ROBERT ORLANDO

Humanix Books

www.humanixbooks.com

Humanix Books

The Tragedy of Patton
Copyright © 2021 by Robert Orlando
All rights reserved

Humanix Books, P.O. Box 20989, West Palm Beach, FL 33416, USA
www.humanixbooks.com | info@humanixbooks.com

No part of this book may be reproduced or transmitted in any form or by any means, electronic or mechanical, including photocopying, recording, or by any other information storage and retrieval system, without written permission from the publisher.

Humanix Books is a division of Humanix Publishing, LLC. Its trademark, consisting of the word "Humanix," is registered in the Patent and Trademark Office and in other countries.

ISBN: 978-1-630-06175-3 (Hardcover)
ISBN: 978-1-630-06176-0 (E-book)

Printed in the United States of America
10 9 8 7 6 5 4 3 2 1

Vincent Orlando, my uncle, US Army SFC, a pilot,
buried at West Point, veteran of World War II,
Korean War, and Vietnam War
January 26, 1925–August 9, 1999

Ralph Orlando, my uncle, US Army, Sergeant, World War II
March 11, 1923–October 9, 2000

Raymond Orlando, my father, Korean War veteran,
who at an early age introduced me to war movies

Contents

Glossary of Names

ALEXANDER THE GREAT (356 BC–323 BC), ruler of the Greek kingdom of Macedonia who set out to rule the world and conquered what is now the Middle East. He was a brilliant military tactician, although that's not all. He was taught by Aristotle and spread Greek culture, beginning the Hellenistic Age. Patton, while commanding the Third Army in Europe, was clearly inspired by Alexander when he wrote the poem "Through a Glass Darkly."

NAPOLEON BONAPARTE (1769–1821), military leader, emperor of France between 1804 and 1814, after which he went into exile on Elba. He was a military genius who conquered most of Europe. Escaping from Elba, he tried to take back power. He was finally, and famously, defeated at Waterloo. During World War II, as the Allies left Africa, British General Sir Harold Alexander told Patton that Napoleon would have made him a marshall if he had been alive in the nineteenth century.

OMAR Nelson BRADLEY (1893–1981), four-star general, commanded the Twelfth Army in World War II, and served as the first chairman of the U.S. Joint Chiefs of Staff. He served under and above Patton. They were joined in their successful mission to defeat the Nazis but differed vastly in style: Patton, charismatic and harsh; Bradley, diligent and compassionate.

JULIUS CAESAR (100 BC–44 BC), general and dictator of Rome, put an end to the Roman Republic but created an empire. Perhaps Patton felt a kinship with this formidable soldier because they both served in Africa and because Caesar also was besieged by self-doubt on occasion.

WINSTON Leonard Spencer-CHURCHILL (1874–1965), army officer, writer, politician who sounded the alarm early and often about the dangers of Nazism's rise. He became prime minister in 1940. As France and other European countries fell, he led the British with unvarnished honesty and soaring words, fighting alone until America finally entered the war.

MARK Wayne CLARK (1896–1984), youngest major general in World War II, promoted to four-star general in 1945, replaced Patton in the 1945 invasion of Italy. He was a controversial figure; he managed with skill—winning over Eisenhower and Churchill—but was disliked by the men under his command.

DWIGHT David EISENHOWER (1890–1969), supreme commander of the Allied Expeditionary Force in Europe, led the D-Day invasion, president of the United States 1953–1961. An affable character who possessed strong administrative and leadership skills. He called on Patton for advice before the Allies hit the Normandy beaches. When news of Patton's mistreatment of soldiers became public, he fired Patton.

JAMES Vincent FORRESTAL (1892–1949), went from Wall Street to Washington, became undersecretary of the Navy and helped build a peacetime navy into a juggernaut. Appointed U.S. secretary of defense in 1947. Like Patton, he was deeply suspicious of Soviet motives and was an important defender of Patton. He died of a reported suicide, which to some observers was suspicious.

LLOYD FREDENDALL (1883–1963), major general, who had more experience training troops than serving in combat. The general in command during the battle of the Kasserine Pass in Tunisia, where Panzer divisions under Gen. Rommel pierced the thin line of Allied troops, leading to the highest casualty rate in World War II. Eisenhower relieved him of command and replaced him with Patton

William AVERELL HARRIMAN (1891–1986), son of a railroad baron, the aristocratic Harriman had a long career in public life as a politician and a diplomat. Franklin Delano Roosevelt appointed him ambassador to the Soviet Union, where he served from 1943 to 1946. His deep knowledge and distrust of Stalin, although noting his wartime prowess as well as his brutality, were only later acknowledged to be right by Roosevelt.

ADOLF HITLER (1889–1945), leader of the Nazi Party, came to power in 1939 when Germany was economically shattered and politically splintered and turned the government into a vicious dictatorship that roiled Europe. The final days of his promised 1,000-year Reich were hastened by Patton's leadership role in the Battle of the Bulge, which Churchill said "will be regarded as an ever-famous American victory."

HARRY Lloyd HOPKINS (1890–1946), New Deal Democrat, FDR's secretary of commerce, became the president's most intimate and trusted adviser. He was the diplomatic back channel to Churchill and was first sent to London in 1941. The prime minister was so taken with Hopkins that he had him stay at 10 Downing Street. Hopkins helped arrange the Potsdam Conference in Moscow. Rumors circulated that he was a communist.

DOUGLAS MacARTHUR (1880–1964), five-star general who commanded the Allies in the Pacific in World War II, accepted the Japanese surrender, was recalled by President Truman when he wanted to widen the war in Korea. He was the only equal of Patton in military brilliance and success. MacArthur did not want Patton in the East, but Patton saluted him in a letter written after they were both in battle in World War I: General MacArthur "never ducked a bullet."

BENITO Amilcare Andrea MUSSOLINI (1883–1945), politician, journalist, head of the fascist party, became Italy's youngest prime minister in 1922. By 1925 he declared himself a dictator, Il Duce. He signed the Pact of Steel with Hitler in 1939. His downfall came in 1943 when Patton led the successful American invasion of Sicily, alongside Britain's troops, led by Gen. Montgomery. In 1945 Italian partisans captured and killed him by firing squad.

BEATRICE Ayer PATTON (1886–1953), the general's wife, daughter of a millionaire, novelist. She was an expert equestrian. Much of what is known about the general's innermost thoughts were revealed in his letters to her, which are included in his diaries. The diaries were entrusted to her and have since been made public.

ERWIN Johannes Eugen ROMMEL (1891–1944), general, hero of World War I, appointed by Hitler to head the Afrika Korps. Authoritative and courageous, he won respect from the Allies and from his men but, like Patton, provoked his superior officers. He was a hero to many Germans, but in the end he ran afoul of Hitler and ended his life with poison.

FRANKLIN Delano ROOSEVELT (1882–1945), governor of New York State, then U.S. president during World War II, forging a bond with his British counterpart Winston Churchill. He lived long enough to see the war end in Europe. Despite Patton's immense contribution to victory, it is presumed that FDR acquiesced in the general's firing by Eisenhower.

WILLIAM Hood SIMPSON (1888–1980), general and commander of the Ninth Army, he led his troops through France, Belgium, and the Netherlands to smash through the Siegfried Line, beating Patton across the Rhine. He was prepared to enter Berlin but was ordered by Eisenhower to hold in place as the Soviets took the city.

JOSEF STALIN (1878–1953), became dictator of the Soviet Union in 1929 and led a brutal regime until his death. He signed a nonaggression pact with Hitler, which among other things was an agreement to carve up Eastern Europe. Hitler betrayed him by invading Russia in 1941. Stalin then formed an uneasy alliance with the United States and Great Britain, helping win the war in the Far East. But the end of World War II was the beginning of the Cold War, something foreseen by Patton.

GEORGY Konstantinovich ZHUKOV (1896–1974), general, deputy commander in chief of the Red Army, responsible for the successful defense of Moscow, Stalingrad, and Leningrad, beating back the German forces, helping to end World War II. Like many in the Union of Soviet Socialist Republics, his fame as a national hero waxed and waned as he fell in and out of favor with Stalin and met his match, verbally, in Patton.

Preface

If everybody is thinking alike,
then somebody isn't thinking.

—General George S. Patton, Jr.

Decades have passed since I first probed General Patton's story and learned of his World War II renown. In the years since, his legacy seems to have faded into the pages of history, as have the vociferous opinions of a general who in his time was loved and hated in equal measure. There is perhaps no greater testament to this paradox than when one of his own men bitterly wondered of Patton, "Won't that old bastard ever get enough of war?" only to later say with beaming pride, "I'm one of Patton's men." Today Patton, like many historical figures, has morphed into a lifeless statue that reflects the political and historical views of our time, not his.

Herein lies the conundrum for the present writer and reader: How do we parse what is contingent and contemporary from what is enduring and ongoing? And how do we observe this nexus between war and our better angels? Is a general in 1944, who slapped soldiers for their perceived lack of courage, a beast, an abuser, or something worse? Whom should we measure him against? Certainly not the enemies he was asked to fight, those who would massacre their opponents without a second thought. So where do we begin when assessing General George S. Patton in light of changing sensibilities on the nature of war and the men who are called to arms?

Consider how many modern works on early American leaders highlight their views on slavery and force those views to the background. Once we conclude that Washington held slaves, does that negate his military acumen? Patton was a general who fought against the most tyrannical empires in modern history and witnessed atrocities that would make current political issues seem laughable by comparison. Perhaps the average college student of today wouldn't focus on the basic context of the twentieth century, let alone the biography of one general. Yet often that same student would be quick to characterize the general as a proto-fascist and warmonger, though it is the soldier himself who knows war and is most hesitant to fight it. Alexander the Great once opined, "For my own part, I would rather excel in knowledge of the highest secrets of philosophy than in arms."

Beyond the campus, Patton has been portrayed in film as having borderline personality disorder. While Patton certainly had a complex psychological profile, complete madmen don't successfully lead liberation armies of hundreds of thousands of soldiers or have the tactical judgment to prepare the contingency plans for offenses like that of the Battle of the Bulge, which staved off Hitler's final attempt at world dominance.

Patton was a tactical genius, well read in both political and military history—a master of his profession. He was a Renaissance man who spoke French, romanticized the gentleman of war, and collected fine wine. He would have followed Napoleon's admonition that

> [w]ar is a serious game, in which one can endanger his
> reputation and his country; a rational man must feel
> and know whether or not he is cut out for this profes-
> sion. Peruse again and again the campaigns of Alexander,

Hannibal, Caesar, Gustavus Adolphus, Turenne, Eugene, and Frederick. Model yourself upon them. This is the only means of becoming a great captain, and of acquiring the secret of the art of war. Your own genius will be enlightened and improved by this study, and you will learn to reject all maxims foreign to the principles of the great commanders.

Patton's ethnic slurs and offensive language were, mainly, well within the mainstream of his day, long before political correctness. Though certainly his antisemitic* diatribes revealed his prejudices, they were not uncommon in his time. As his biographer, Martin Blumenson, observes, "He jumped from vulgarity to scholarship as nimbly as a cat."

The scope of this biography eschews the need to explain Patton in the ready-made political categories of our time and reveals a common trait of great leaders: He was an enigmatic man who could not live up to the myth, an imperfect man who, in the end, would be judged by his mission, as are all great men. Indeed, it was Alexander who said, "In the end, when it's over, all that matters is what you've done." And another Patton hero, George Washington, is judged for his decision to surprise the Hessians in defiance of a king and his army and his step away from his offer to be emperor.

As biographer James Flexner offers in his introduction to *Washington, The Indispensable Man*:

---

* I adopt Doris Bergen's justification for this spelling of *antisemitism*: "Often you will see the word written with a hyphen—'anti-Semitism'[. . . .] Use of the hyphen implies that there was such a thing as 'Semitism,' which antisemites opposed. In fact, those who used the term in the nineteenth century (and since) have understood it to refer only to hostility toward Jews." Doris L. Bergen, *War and Genocide: A Concise History of the Holocaust*, 3rd ed. (Lanham, MD: Rowman & Littlefield, 2016), 15.

[A]lmost every historical figure is regarded as a dead exemplar of a vanished epoch. But Washington exists within the minds of most Americans as an active force. He is a multitude of living ghosts, each shaped less by eighteenth-century reality than by the structure of the individual brain in which he dwells. An inhabitant of intimate spaces, Washington is for private reason sought out or avoided, loved or admired, hated or despised. I have come across almost no Americans who prove, when the subject is really broached, emotionally indifferent to George Washington.

What of Patton's role in history? This flawed man led American forces across North Africa and broke through the deadlock after the Normandy invasion—actions that speak for themselves and are an essential part of completing a Patton portrait. They are well known to historians. There is no mystery as to his military prowess. He had within his grasp the capture of Berlin and Prague but was held back by senior leadership, with disastrous results.

Patton, when compared with the classic archetypes of mythical construction, could be seen as a modern Ajax, with all the gifts and flaws of a tragic antihero. Like Ajax, Patton was one who surpassed most in his originality, intelligence, and sheer force of physical vitality. He was equally undermined by flaws—or, in modern parlance, blind spots—of vanity and an inability to fully embrace how his statesmanship could be dangerous to the morale of a democratic people struggling to hold a moral boundary in a time of war. In his studies, military historian Victor Davis Hanson identifies Patton as an updated form of the antihero, as seen in modern westerns like *Shane* or *The Wild Bunch*. Like his cinematic counterparts, Patton is the one who is called in when there is no longer the means to protect the village with conventional justice. What's needed is someone on the outskirts of genteel society. Someone who might cause a moral blush in peaceful times but seduces a necessary attraction when violence is at America's door or on the doorsteps of our allies facing the Nazis.

Moreover, Patton is forged out of a type of premodern rock from an earlier age where artifacts such as manliness and the role as leader or U.S. general would come after a life of study and the practice of wearing the mask of command. His mask was not false in the emotional transparency of the modern world but fashioned for the vital reason that the nation was being defined by war— an understanding that could have been gleaned from Patton's own military library. From the ancient Greeks to modern times, as a culture evolves to a leisure class, one fatigued by war, Patton's type is recast as an enemy of democracy, especially when calling out the emerging Soviet empire. Ironic since Stalin would have dismissed such notions as tripe. Patton had a trained ancient soul of war but needed to function on a democratic stage.

In his book *Patton: A Genius for War*, biographer Carlo D'Este describes the challenge of

> how to motivate decent young men raised on the precepts of the Bible, the sanctity of human life, and the immorality of killing to become an efficient cog in a gigantic killing machine such as an armored division. While it was enough to make their mothers cringe, the only method whereby a Patton . . . could succeed on a battlefield was to trespass on the inherent decency of Americans by training and motivating their men to survive by killing others whose task was to kill them. Patton did it as well or better than virtually anyone else.

But there is a final chapter to his life that is lesser known and is often lost in the retelling of World War II. It was after the war's end, when he was assigned as governor of Bavaria and asked to transform himself from battlefield leader of thousands of troops to an administrator juggling the mundane tasks of waste management, utilities provision, and population control. Here we find a hidden chapter: Patton had ideas of what to do in the war's aftermath, warning that the Soviets would pick up exactly where the Nazis had left off. He no longer had the guns to win battles, but he had a microphone, his rhetoric, and his instincts. Repeatedly, however, his microphone was turned off. He was commanded to be quiet. Why? Why were we so threatened by a prescient patriot who was *TIME* magazine's Man of the Year? What made his insights so dangerous that many have come to believe his accidental death might not have been an accident? The purpose of this book is to dig deep and, as Hamlet said, "delve one yard below their mines," beneath the binary categories of today's politics, and to explode retrograde righteousness for its lack of perspective and unwillingness to embrace human complexity.

When we hear adamant and abrasive voices like Patton's, we have a choice. We can change the channel and consign them to the rantings of racists, ascendant white European males, and the "unenlightened" of an earlier time. Or we can be courageous enough to recognize that the wheels of time grind in circles, and what seems only of the past will soon come around again. And that time might require a not-so-polished leader to redirect our peacetime sensibilities. Better to learn and prepare than to deny and hope.

As a general, Patton measured himself against the military legends of antiquity. Indeed, from an early age, he was moved by the words of Thucydides from his chronicling of the "Funeral Oration of Pericles" in *The History of the Peloponnesian War*:

> For the whole earth is the tomb of famous men; not only
> are they commemorated by columns and inscriptions in
> their own country, but in foreign lands there dwells also

an unwritten memorial of them, graven not on stone but in the hearts of men. Make them your examples, and, esteeming courage to be freedom and freedom to be happiness, do not weigh too nicely the perils of war.

Patton would have appreciated similar sentiments on his own tombstone and would allow his own life to speak for itself. But the study of history, he believed, was not merely for the sake of understanding and informing, as is apparent from the library he amassed and consulted religiously. Rather, he believed what Alfred Thayer Mahan writes in *The Influence of Sea Power Upon History, 1660–1783*, "The study of history lies at the foundation of all sound military conclusions and practice." But it was not solely an intellectual knowledge that motivated Patton. As military historian John Keegan writes, there is a distinction between an intellect and a leader: "Mankind, if it is to survive, must choose its leaders by the test of their intellectuality; and, contrarily, leadership must justify itself by its detachment, moderation and power of analysis."

At key moments in Patton's career, he was prevented from fulfilling his duty. At certain times, the pauses would also delay his crafted destiny. The narrative that follows is by no means an exhaustive biography of what many historians consider to be the twentieth century's most brilliant and controversial American general. Many fine scholars have already looked closely at the history and character of this quintessential military leader. Rather, this account focuses narrowly on the personal qualities and wartime events that prompted senior military command to repeatedly rein in and quiet its most prescient warrior. And finally, the account ahead explores how these matters would alter the legacy Patton believed he deserved and the extraordinary destiny he vigorously pursued.

Prologue

It is foolish and wrong to mourn the men who died.
Rather we should thank God that such men lived.

—GENERAL GEORGE S. PATTON, JR.
Speech at the Copley Plaza Hotel,
Boston, Massachusetts, June 7, 1945

It is December 9, 1945, seven months since the end of the war in Europe. On a war-torn two-lane highway in Mannheim, Germany, the most formidable and audacious American commander of World War II, Gen. George S. Patton, and the two other occupants of his Cadillac, Maj. General Hobart Gay and Pfc. Horace L. Woodring, have stopped at a railroad crossing to wait for a train to pass. In the silence, Patton remarked, "How awful war is. Think of the waste."

The sedan continues a few hundred yards, passing a quartermaster depot. Something suspicious captures Patton's attention. He is seated in the rear of the vehicle, perched at the edge of his seat. Could this have been—as so many have thought—a hidden gunman? A would-be assassin? Woodring, who is behind the wheel, turns to look at the object of Patton's interest. In that instant, a 2.5-ton Army truck, driven by Sgt. Robert L. Thompson, suddenly makes a sharp left in front of the staff car. Despite Woodring's best efforts, the truck and staff car collide.

Remarkably, Patton is dazed but still conscious after the impact. Through gritted teeth, he quips, "Christ, what a way to start a leave." Patton has a broken neck. He is paralyzed from the neck down. The other occupants of the vehicle walk away from the accident unscathed, but "Old Blood and Guts" would cling to life in a Heidelberg hospital. Within two weeks, Patton is dead—an inauspicious end for a man who believed his destiny was to lead the world's greatest army in the world's greatest war and die, in his own words, as "the last man from the last bullet."

"He never thought he would die in peacetime let alone in an accident," observes military historian Victor Davis Hanson. "Patton saw himself going back from Europe as a conquering hero. He certainly did not see himself going back encased in plaster as a quadriplegic."

But why is Patton the only one to sustain serious injury in the collision? Suspiciously, there is no autopsy after he dies.

Was this a freak accident, or were more sinister forces at play? If so, who would want to kill America's greatest general? Patton had vowed to "take the gag off" after the war and tell the intimate truth about controversial decisions and questionable politics that had cost the lives of his men. He threatened a war with the Russians and disobeyed orders by keeping a German army intact for that purpose. Could these pledges to "out" his wartime rivals and even friends in Berlin, Moscow, and Washington have been the cause of this supposed accident? Were those who held Patton's fate in their hands afraid of what they saw as his threat to world peace? After 75 years, the mystery remains, but perhaps now, by looking more closely at Patton's own memoirs and those of his rivals and at Josef Stalin's influence over FDR, Churchill, and the agreements establishing the postwar order, the mystery can be solved.

....

CHAPTER ONE

The Soul of a Warrior

Human nature loves a hero—the good guy in the white hat who takes the moral high ground and possesses all the appropriate and desirable virtues, like honor, courage, and integrity. Heroes are the folks who do the right thing at the right time for the right reasons. In general, these are the figures we look to for leadership. And in the best of times, heroes get the job done and are admired for it.

But there is another sort of character, rough around the edges, irascible at times, more practical than virtuous. This is the antihero. Often the antihero lacks the sort of polish or refined qualities we like to assign to a hero. In fact, the antihero can be downright annoying, obnoxious, and offensive—a real boor. Yet, in certain circumstances—most especially war—an antihero is what's needed. General George S. Patton was America's antihero of World War II.

Patton had a clear-eyed understanding of the nature of war. Victor Davis Hanson describes the Patton mentality this way:

> If you feel you are going to risk the collective use of your country for an existential cause, you have to defeat the enemy by killing more of them than you. You have to destroy their ability to make war. You have to occupy their territory. You have to submit terms for them. Then you

have to reconfigure their politics so that they are a friend or at least a neutral. That dates back to the Greeks. We forget that [maxim] the more careful, the more educated, the more nuanced we become. So, then we get into a jam, and suddenly, where are the generals?

Patton was simultaneously brilliant and deeply flawed. He was daring and noble on occasion, like the Greek and Roman military legends he revered. At other times he was petulant and cruel, lacking in the diplomatic grace and tact that defined many of his contemporaries, a real son-of-a-bitch. Patton was the kind of guy the Allies needed to get the dirty work done on the ground but also the guy they wanted to get rid of once the fighting was over.

The Stage

In the early autumn of 1945, just months after the end of hostilities in the European theater, Gen. Eisenhower was confronted by fallout from remarks made by the fearless but brash Patton. On September 22, Patton, now military governor of Bavaria, had met with reporters. In Martin Blumenson's *The Patton Papers 1940–1945*, we learn that, when pressed, he had not removed a German official who was a known critic of the American denazification program, Patton compared the denazification program to a foreign power, having conquered the United States, removing Republicans and Democrats from office. This remark, which Patton later asserted was taken out of context, was construed to mean that Patton viewed the Nazi Party as analogous to the Democratic or Republican parties, thereby sparking a firestorm of criticism by the press.

Patton was increasingly alarmed by the looming threat of Russian troops amassing in Eastern Europe because he considered the Soviet threat to be much greater than that of the Nazis regaining power. He was convinced that with the Third Reich defeated, American policy should address what he viewed as the United States' true enemy: the Soviet Union. Patton, no stranger to the blaze of the spotlight or the sting of popular criticism, believed it was his job to tell the world. Eisenhower, who had never fought a battle, had become the master of diplomacy, usually leaving other officers to take the strong stands. Yet now he was out of options—after repeated offenses, he had to cut Patton's microphone due to his incendiary opinions, though Ike himself had expressed similar sentiments earlier. Apparently, something behind the scenes had changed Eisenhower's opinion.

This was not the first time Patton had caused trouble for his superiors. Throughout the course of World War II, he had openly expressed his opinions, especially when he disagreed with official policy. But contrary to popular belief, Patton was not always so defiant, nor was he simply a lover of violence or a blustering warmonger. Indeed, in his early years, he complied with authority without any real trouble, but Patton's opinions multiplied as his place in the world ascended higher and higher, until at last, he flew too close to the sun. There was nothing inevitable about this result, however. To grasp how he reached that point, it is critical to understand how he first took flight.

The Early Years

George Smith Patton, Jr., was born on November 11, 1885, in San Gabriel, California. His doting parents, George Sr. and Ruth Wilson, provided a comfortable, nurturing environment for their son. The Pattons were well-off, and "Georgie," as he was called, was descended from a long line of military men. As Martin Blumenson notes in *Patton: The Man Behind the Legend*, Patton was haunted by "several sets of ghosts" throughout his lifetime, including his

martial ancestors, the great men of history and literature, and figures from his early years, especially relatives. As far as Patton saw it,
his chief duty in life was to live up to—if not surpass—the military
precedent set by his forebears. With his comfortable upbringing
and obsession with his filial duty, Patton's early years are, as Dennis
Showalter in *Patton and Rommel* puts it, a story of "a prince asserting his heritage."

While Patton had a comfortable, if not aristocratic, childhood,
his development from boy to man was not without adversity. For
example, as a young boy—and indeed, for his whole life—Patton
suffered from what would later be called dyslexia and attention
deficit disorder, or ADD. Some biographers of Patton, such as
Stanley P. Hirshon, argue that Patton was not dyslexic, but rather
that the informal education he received from his Aunt Nannie for
the first 12 years of his life explained his deficient spelling. The
reason why Patton did not know how to read or write until he
was 12 years old, Hirshon argues, is because his aunt and father
would read aloud to him. Rather than first learning how to read
and write words, Patton was instructed by a former Confederate
cavalry officer, John Singleton Mosby, in how to read and work
with maps. Hirshon asserts that Patton's report cards from Stephen
Cutter Clark's Classical School for Boys in Pasadena, California,
confirm this theory, citing his arithmetic and spelling grades as evidence that Patton did not suffer from dyslexia. As far as arithmetic
scores go, Hirshon simply posits in *General Patton*—in contrast to
other Patton biographers—that Patton's fluctuating performance in
that subject is evidence "that he did not consistently have trouble
with mathematics, as those who call him dyslexic assert." While
Patton's scores reveal that he certainly did not consistently struggle
with math, he most certainly did not consistently succeed in that
subject; indeed, the fluctuation in his performance suggests that he
had trouble retaining certain mathematical concepts.

Hirshon's argument regarding Patton's spelling grades—that he "had no difficulty spelling words given to him, leading to the conclusion that his spelling troubles stemmed from learning to read and write six or seven years after his fellow students"—is more plausible, but there are still deficiencies, given that "[o]nce [Patton] learned to read, he read incessantly," a trait that, under normal circumstances, would ostensibly improve his spelling. Indeed, as psychiatrist Gerald W. Grumet notes: "there are many variants of dyslexia, and one milder type is characterized by excellent reading skills but poor spelling. This is an impairment which poses no problem in recognizing written words . . . but the person struggles with the reverse process of spelling a known word."

Patton, Grumet argues, likely struggled with this variant of dyslexia and would today be classified as a "Type B Speller." As such, it seems that the view of most Patton biographers that the general was dyslexic holds up under scrutiny.

Patton was self-conscious about his conditions, not least because his classmates often mocked him for his struggles in reading aloud or showing his work on the classroom chalkboard. Despite these challenges, Patton pushed himself in his studies and became well read, though his penchant for poor spelling and even poorer penmanship haunted him his whole life. After an abortive campaign to earn an appointment to the U.S. Military Academy at West Point from a local senator, Patton matriculated to Virginia Military Institute, or VMI, in autumn 1903.

For all his life, Patton was a markedly insecure man, petrified by the notion of failing to live up to the standards of his pedigree. When he confided in his uncle that he feared he might be a coward, his uncle reassured him that "no Patton could be a coward," meaning that when push came to shove, young George would stand his ground and triumph, or die trying—a sentiment he would later convey to his own men. The young "rat"—a term for first-year VMI cadets—muddled his way through freshman year and attempted once more to earn an appointment to the U.S. Military Academy. This time Patton secured the appointment and began attending West Point in 1904. Despite some initial struggles in his studies, which resulted in him being held back a year, Patton eventually found his bearings, and though only ever an average student at West Point, he excelled both in athletics and in climbing the ranks among his fellow cadets, as he quickly became the adjutant of his regiment. He graduated in 1909 and entered the cavalry, indicative of his obsession with the offensive in combat, which came to characterize his military career. As Roger Nye writes in *The Patton Mind*, "He had acquired a sense of discipline and devotion to duty but had maintained his sense of individualism and uniqueness in the crowd about him." Not only had Patton completed his education at West Point, but he had also become an avid reader in the process, eager to learn as much as he could about his craft.

He joined the Fifteenth Cavalry at Fort Sheridan, Illinois, where he soon made his mark as a commander. Once, after mistakenly yelling "damn you," rather than "damn it" at a subordinate, he publicly apologized to his men, much to their amusement and delight. It was right that Patton apologized to his men for his words, and he would become intimately familiar with the practice throughout the course of his career. In light of Patton's later, rougher approach to dealing with his men—what one might call "tough love"—however, this episode is highly ironic.

Patton married his childhood sweetheart, Beatrice Ayer, in March 1910. Their daughter, also named Beatrice, was born the following year. As numerous Patton biographers relate, the soldier was quite jealous of his own children, as they took up much of Beatrice's time.

In 1912, Patton represented the United States at the Olympic Games in Stockholm, Sweden, where he competed in the first modern pentathlon, placing fifth. After the games, Patton spent time in France, where he studied the language and French cavalry doctrine and trained with the world's greatest fencing master, Adj. M. Cléry. It was during this time that Patton first expressed his belief in reincarnation on paper, saying he believed he had fought in France in previous lives, a claim he would later repeat. In a letter to his mother, written while he was in Chamlieu, France, he wrote on November 20, 1917:

> I wonder if I could have been here before as I drive up the Roman road the Theater seems familiar—perhaps I headed a legion up that same white road. . . . I passed a chateau in ruins which I possibly helped escalade in the middle ages. There is no proof nor yet any denial. We were, we are, and we will be.

Profanity and Prayer

Patton was a man of faith but one full of extremes and blatant contradictions. On the one hand, he was a professing Episcopalian with ecumenical views and was generally orthodox in his beliefs. On the other hand, Patton read the texts of other religions (e.g., the Qur'an and Bhagavad Gita), protested his daughter marrying a Roman Catholic, and freely mixed profanity into his religious convictions. Once, U.S. Rep. Clare Booth Luce asked him, "General, do you read the Bible?" and Patton responded, "Every goddamned day."

More striking than Patton's profane approach to his faith was his firm belief in reincarnation, as noted in Michael Keane's *Blood, Guts, and Prayer*. From a very young age, Patton had professed his conviction that he could recall memories from past lives, when he had been a soldier, whether as a caveman, a Roman legionary, a Viking, or one of Napoleon's marshals. This belief seemingly stemmed, at least in part, from the influence of family members, who held a number of unorthodox—if not heterodox—beliefs. For example, his maternal grandmother had allegedly sensed every time that her husband had been wounded in the Civil War, prior to receiving news of his injuries. Similarly, Patton's "Papa," George Sr., had a keen interest in "the science of prediction and used the measurements of the Great Pyramid of Cheops for his prophecies," as noted in Blumenson's *The Man Behind the Legend.* Other relatives, including Patton's sister, had "psychic experiences" involving dead relatives. Another factor in Patton's belief in reincarnation was his extensive knowledge of military history. As Martin Blumenson writes, the stories of old "induced in him a strain of mysticism, a sense of déjà vu, an acceptance of telepathy, and a belief in reincarnation. . . . [Patton] turned to history as a means of understanding the present and foretelling the future." It is worth noting here that in the nineteenth and early twentieth centuries, unorthodox religious beliefs, such as spiritualism, theosophy, and the like, were highly fashionable in the upper echelons of society.

Only some of Patton's closest friends and family members knew about his belief in reincarnation, likely because it was still considered relatively taboo, especially in Christian circles. Interestingly, while one of Patton's justifications for his belief in reincarnation came—unsurprisingly—from the Bhagavad Gita, a Hindu holy text, another defense he used was Revelation 3:12: "Him that overcometh will I make a pillar in the temple of my God, and he shall go out no more." This verse was seemingly interpreted by Patton to mean that he could earn a higher place in Heaven through his military exploits, which, as Carlo D'Este writes, sprang from Patton's concern "that he attain immortality by fulfilling his destiny of becoming a great military leader during this particular lifetime." At the same time, Patton seemingly expected—and wanted—this cycle of birth, life, death, and rebirth as a warrior to continue in perpetuum. D'Este continues, arguing that "Patton was not concerned with the ultimate end of the cycle of birth and death; he merely wanted to continue life as yet another warrior." So set was Patton on fulfilling his destiny of becoming a legendary commander that, as a young man, he wrote in his diary, "If you do not die a soldier and having had a chance to be one I pray to God to dam [sic] you George Patton."

Patton was fixated on the notion of reaching the status of a military legend and driven by outdated notions about honor, drawing from the Greek concept of *aretē* and medieval notions of chivalry, both of which had received a heightened level of attention in the 1800s. Historian Victor Davis Hanson aptly describes Patton as "a clearly anachronistic figure who belonged more to the nineteenth century of his birth" and who "functioned in a modern society that he scarcely understood." He "enjoyed killing enemy soldiers because he felt them to be agents of evil and a danger to a democratic society," which, in Hanson's estimation, encompassed "the soul of battle."

As a prolific writer of poetry, Patton's syncretic beliefs left their mark on his writings. For example, in his 1922 poem, "Through a Glass Darkly," Patton recounts his many past lives as a warrior, even musing that "Perhaps I stabbed our Savior / In His sacred helpless side. / Yet I've called His name in blessing / When in after times I died." Patton's syncretism is striking, though he seemed comfortable with the tension between his beliefs.

Despite his unorthodox beliefs, Patton also had a fairly orthodox faith in many regards. For example, he believed in the power of prayer, saying that it was "like plugging in on a current whose source is in Heaven. . . . [It] completes the circuit. It is power." His faith in communing with the Divine was not a cynical means by which to inspire his men, however. Rather, he sincerely believed he had a spiritual responsibility toward his soldiers and regularly emphasized the importance of prayer and good preaching in the units he commanded, as seen in his insistence on the distribution of pamphlets on the importance of prayer.

Patton's complex personality was perhaps best described by his colleague and rival, Omar Bradley, who wrote in *A Soldier's Story* that the "contradictions in Patton's character . . . bewilder[ed] his staff. For while he was profane, he was also reverent. And while he strutted imperiously as a commander, he knelt humbly before his God." And while he was prone to "hammy gesture[s]" in his pre-battle speeches, they "helped to make it more clearly apparent . . . that to Patton[,] war was a holy crusade." Bradley might have confronted Patton's unbridled arrogance with the words of Clausewitz, "Vanity is content with the appearance alone."

From Cavalryman to Tanker

Upon returning from France, Patton continued his quest for promotion, eagerly taking the opportunity to dine with Secretary of War Henry Stimson and Army Chief of Staff Leonard Wood and expanding his social circle to include major generals and other high-ranking officers. His prestige increased as he published articles in military journals. These articles reflected his interests in history, training, and especially the use of the saber. In his anonymously authored essay, "Use of the Point in Sword Play," Patton critiqued the American cavalry saber as inefficient because it was a curved blade that relied on slashing, rather than a straight blade used for thrusting with the point, as the French did. So effectively did Patton argue for an "enclosed" model saber that the Army commissioned 20,000 manufactured according to his design. These weapons, which came to be known as "Patton swords," were, unfortunately for the young first lieutenant, soon to be outmoded, as the notion of using cavalry in combat was exploded by the trench warfare of World War I, which ushered in the era of machine guns, mass artillery bombardments, aircraft, and—most significantly for Patton—tanks.

When World War I broke out in late 1914, Patton petitioned Gen. Wood to permit him to go to the Continent to join a French cavalry unit led by a personal friend. Given the United States' official position of neutrality, Wood denied Patton's request, saying that the only role in which he would permit him to be involved in the conflict was as an observer, which was unconscionable to the eager young officer.

Despite this disappointing development, Patton had another opportunity to distinguish himself two years later, in his first active deployment during the Punitive Expedition to Mexico in 1916, led by Gen. John "Black Jack" Pershing. The expedition aimed to eliminate the threat of Mexican revolutionary leader Pancho Villa, whose raids into the southern United States had exacerbated tensions between the United States and Mexico. Patton served as Pershing's aide, and in addition to finding food and lodging for his boss, he also managed Pershing's schedule and assumed various administrative duties for him.

Patton distinguished himself by leading an attack that killed Julio Cárdenas, the head of Villa's personal guard, los Dorados (the Golden Ones), named for the gold on their shirt sleeve fringes. The young lieutenant, upon learning that Cárdenas was nearby, requested permission to track him down. Upon receiving the go-ahead, Patton led Troop C of the Thirteenth Cavalry to the town of San Miguel, where Cárdenas's uncle, wife, and child were hiding. After torturing Cárdenas's uncle proved fruitless—Patton described him as "a very brave man and nearly died before he would tell me anything"—Patton set up some of his men to stake out the house and rejoined the Thirteenth Cavalry.

Almost two weeks later, while out buying corn with some of his men, Patton's guide, a former Villista, recognized some of his old comrades and alerted Patton. After revisiting the house, where the uncle seemed uneasy, Patton took his detachment of 14 men—four of them civilians—to Mrs. Cárdenas's ranch in San Miguelito. Sure enough, her husband was also there and was killed in a shootout that lasted 15 minutes. It was in this attack that Patton became the first—and for a time, the only—American officer to use auto-mobiles in an offensive military capacity. The raid earned him national acclaim, with some dubbing him "the Bandit Killer." It wasn't merely the kills that earned him renown; it was the fact that, following the encounter, he strapped the dead bodies to the hood of his car, invoking the imagery of a great hunter. When news first broke of his accomplishments, a neighbor shouted to Patton's wife, "Your husband's a Medal of Honor man now, Mrs. Patton."

On April 6, 1917, the United States officially declared war on Germany, thereby giving Patton his first opportunity to engage a trained enemy—after all, the Punitive Expedition was an asym-metric conflict against rebels, not trained soldiers. Pershing, who commanded the American Expeditionary Force (AEF), brought Patton, now a captain, along with him to manage his headquarters in France. Soon enough, Patton was introduced to the tank, which had been developed by the British and the French, as they sought to hold off the massive German army. Around this time, the ambitious young officer grew increasingly discontented with his lot; indeed, he described his role under Pershing as being "nothing but [a] hired flunky" and burned with desire to see action. During a hospital visit for jaundice in October 1917, Patton was advised by his roommate to find a way into another position, unaffiliated with Pershing, for the sake of his career, since he could not hope for advancement in his present role. He wrote to Beatrice, saying, "There is a lot of talk about 'Tanks' here now, and I am interested as I can see no future in my present job." But Patton was unsure where his talents would be best used. Should he enter the infantry or the tanks? Perhaps he could train soldiers to use the bayonet. Eventually, his friends and peers pushed him toward working with tanks.

One of the critical influencers in Patton's decision was Col. Paul B. Malone, with whom he had become friends at Fort Sheridan. Malone was in the process of establishing the First Army Tank School and urged Patton to apply for a position as a training officer there. While some of his friends warned against such a move, arguing that the infantry was less of a risk in terms of chances for promotion, Patton recognized the new technology's tremendously high ceiling. If he could demonstrate the efficacy of tanks to his superiors, he could ascend rapidly in both rank and historical significance. As such, he decided in November 1917 to apply for an appointment to the tank school.

In his petition to Pershing, Patton argued that his track record with using automobiles in an offensive capacity during the Punitive Expedition qualified him for tank service. Furthermore, while the British considered tanks to be the land equivalent of gunboats—the Royal Navy had led the charge in developing tanks—and the French viewed them as mobile artillery—an artilleryman, Col. J. B. Estienne, led French tank development—Patton conceived of tanks as modern cavalry. This created a variety of possible combat uses for the new weapon. Pershing approved Patton's request, and the young officer made his way to the French Light Tank Training Center on November 18, thus beginning his transition from a soon-to-be-obsolete cavalryman into an officer on the cutting edge of the military technology that came to define his career.

Patton took to the tank instantly, driving one on his very first day at the training center. His first combat experience with tanks involved the Renault model, a small, light vehicle weighing in at a mere 6.5 tons. (The modern M1 Abrams tank weighs 65 to 72 tons.) On that very day, the British had successfully employed the new technology at the Battle of Cambrai (November 20–December 8), leading to a frenzy in the Army, as officers and men scrambled to gain appointments to tank units. Patton had joined at precisely the right time. He was so invested in the new technology that while touring the Renault factory, he made several recommendations to improve the light tank, and the designers ultimately adopted them all.

Though it took until March 1918 for his tanks to finally arrive, Patton distinguished himself and brought attention to the utility of tanks through his leadership in the Battle of Saint-Mihiel (September 12–15) and the Meuse-Argonne Offensive (September 26–November 11). From the beginning, Patton led his men from the front, rather than staying safely behind them, despite his superiors' advice to the contrary. To manage this, he conceived of a system of message runners and carrier pigeons, which allowed him to remain in contact with the rear while operating on the front lines. Having realized that ducking and dodging would do little to protect him from death, Patton regularly exposed himself to enemy fire while leading his men. Doubtless part of his inspiration for such heroics came from his encounter with then–Brig. Gen. Douglas MacArthur, with whom he stood on a small hill while an artillery barrage crept toward them during the Battle of Saint-Mihiel. When he noticed Patton flinch, MacArthur reassured him, saying, "Don't worry, major; you never hear the one that gets you."

Coincidentally, Patton "found his bullet" just a few days later. Near Cheppy on the first day of the Meuse-Argonne Offensive, Patton, having abandoned his tank, found a group of tankers sitting in a trench rather than destroying it to facilitate the passage of their vehicles. While he stood atop the trench, yelling at them, they begged him to get down, saying he could be shot. He refused, declaring "To Hell, [sic] with them—they can't hit me." Shortly thereafter, he rallied some infantrymen to press toward the enemy, swinging his walking stick wildly above his head. While they charged up a hill at a German machine gun nest, Patton was shot in the buttocks and collapsed, thereafter commanding the remainder of that engagement from a foxhole before going to a field hospital. Though he returned to active service in late October, he did not see any more combat in World War I. By the end of that conflict, however, he had distinguished himself enough to be promoted to colonel. He was awarded the Distinguished Service Cross and, a little over a decade later, the Purple Heart, both for his conduct at Cheppy.

Though Patton's actions at Cheppy won him several awards and a promotion, the incident meant much more to him than the recognition of his fellow man. He vindicated himself as a Patton on that day, as he demonstrated that he was unafraid to engage the enemy, no matter the conditions. He was petrified during the action, but this experience helped him understand the true meaning of courage: not being fearless but being able to overcome fear. It was a sort of "mountaintop experience" for the young warrior, as seen in his dramatic retelling of the story in 1927:

> Just before I was wounded I felt a great desire to run, I
> was trembling with fear when suddenly I thought of my
> progenitors and seemed to see them in a cloud over the
> German lines looking at me. I became calm at once and
> saying out loud "It is time for another Patton to die"
> called for volunteers and went forward to what I honestly
> believed to be certain death. Six men went with me; five
> were killed and I was wounded so I was not much in error.

For Patton, then, his conduct in World War I was a sign of his ability to be the consummate warrior, one who could remain calm while being shelled, shot at, or wounded. He had proven he had courage worthy of the family name. But at the heart of Patton's courage was a basic fear. At Cheppy, Patton was driven by the almost-suicidal urge to prove himself worthy of his surname. If he were not to succeed in the contest of arms, he at least would ensure his death in battle so that he could not be disdained as a coward by his ancestors. Combat was, for Patton, the means by which to attain glory befitting both his ancestral heritage and his eventual legacy. Indeed, when the war ended on November 11, 1918, which was Patton's thirty-third birthday, he was disappointed. After his injury, he had written Beatrice, saying, "Peace looks possible, but I rather hope not for I would like to have a few more fights." In his poem "Peace—November 11, 1918," Patton relates how his "heart shrank in dismay" because he knew it would be some time until he would "[know] once more the whitehot joy / Of taking human life."

Patton's description of killing as "whitehot joy" is certainly unsettling and sounds rather like something a warmonger or a sociopath might write. Indeed, the psychology of killers—whether murderers, terrorists, or special operations personnel—is often far different from that of "normal" people. These differences are often related to an enlarged hypothalamus, which makes its possessor more prone to violence. It is important to note, however, that though Patton was certainly not afraid of killing, he was no sadist and did not prolong the suffering of his enemies. While he took pleasure in killing, he did so because he saw his enemies as representing a great evil that could not be permitted to linger on the Earth. Indeed, just as both murderers and Navy SEALs have enlarged hypothalami—making it a question of how one channels one's violent tendencies—so too was Patton's aggressive nature a boon in time of war.

His emotional volatility made him more vulnerable in his relationships with others, especially his men, and that concerned him greatly. In Europe, he wept as he kissed the heads of his wounded men while brutally slapping those men whose wounds were mental. One night, six years before his first landing against the Axis forces, his eldest son, George, walked into his study and found him crying.

Patton had been reading *Generalship: Its Diseases and Their Cure* (1933) by J. F. C. Fuller, which listed the greatest military commanders in history and their greatest wars. Patton was crestfallen when he realized he was older than almost all of those seminal leaders when they had their grandest achievements.

At the end of the book, Fuller provides an appendix with an extensive list of the greatest 100 generals. The section opens with Fuller writing, "The following list is unprejudiced by any idea of proving youth to be itself a military virtue." He continues, "The interesting points to note are: that according to this list the average age, or zenith of generalship is 40.36 years; that 74% of the generals mentioned are forty-five years old or under; and that only 4% are sixty or over."

Clearly Patton considered his life in terms of his comparisons, but he was in good company with the likes of Julius Caesar, who was saddened by his comparison with Alexander. Plutarch writes:

> So, when Caesar read about Alexander's life, he burst into tears. Perhaps the more ambitious of us ought to cry with him. His friends were surprised and asked him the reason of it. "Do you think," said he, "I have not just cause to weep, when I consider that Alexander at my age had conquered so many nations, and I have all this time done nothing that is memorable?"

During the interwar period, Patton worked to develop tank doctrine, pursued further education at West Point, and was moved around the country, stationed at various posts in Hawaii, Massachusetts, Texas, and the District of Columbia. He continued to distinguish himself in peacetime but wrote to Pershing in 1919, "war is the only place where a man really lives." He threw himself into expanding his already prodigious military skills, advancing the art of armored warfare, developing strong relationships with key military leaders, and even designing new military uniforms for tank operators. It was as if (as Poe wrote in "The Raven") "perfumed from an unseen censer" he sensed he must prepare for a destiny beyond his sight. Meanwhile, back in Europe, an Austrian-born corporal in the German army began wondering what it might be like to rule the world.

Patton did not have an easy time outside of his assignments in war and especially during the interwar years. Many have speculated whether Patton's mental struggles during this time were a result of depression, an earlier equestrian injury, or his dyslexia, which resulted in his erratic behavior. Historian Daniel Crosswell argued that "Patton was mad. Not barking at the moon or falling down and eating the rug mad, but mad nonetheless." According to Crosswell, Patton's condition was the result of a bipolar condition inherited from his father.

Military historian Carlo D'Este would counter by noting Patton's well-known dyslexia, a disorder that could also contribute to his induced mood swings and rash statements. And more important, a common trait of dyslexics is low self-esteem, which plagued Patton his entire life. Yet, even if these factors did contribute to his level of frustration, they cannot explain how this same man would later emerge, according to Gen. Eisenhower, as the greatest field general of World War II.

Patton left France in March 1919. After the war, he was assigned to Camp Meade, Maryland, where he developed his opinion that tanks should be used not as infantry support but rather as an independent fighting force. He supported the M1919 tank design created by J. Walter Christie, a project that was shelved due to financial considerations.

Patton first met Eisenhower in 1919 while on duty in Washington, DC. The two began a long-standing correspondence and, along with J. Walter Christie and assorted other officers, pushed for more development of armored warfare during the inter-war era. While the recommendations resonated with then–Secretary of War Dwight Davis, the limited military budget and prevalence of already-established infantry and cavalry branches meant the United States would not develop its armored corps until much later in 1940.

In the prelude to World War II, Patton continued his train-ing and his climb up the ranks. He developed concepts for mecha-nized warfare and was assigned an assortment of commands, but he loathed his duties as a peacetime officer. Patton continued building his relationship with Eisenhower, who wrote: "From the beginning he and I got along famously. Both of us were students of current military doctrine. Part of our passion was our belief in tanks—a belief derided at the time by others." Both shared a detailed knowl-edge of the mechanical workings of tanks and an appreciation of their potential strategic uses beyond mere assistance to the infantry. Patton was being designed for battle.

Patton also first demonstrated his aptitude for prophecy during the Sino-Japanese War, which began in July 1937, as he warned of a potential Japanese surprise attack against the United States. Unfortunately, his warning was ignored, and the report was filed away. It would not be the last time his premonitions fell on deaf ears. Even so, Patton's warning proved well founded when the Japanese attacked Pearl Harbor on December 7, 1941. The dismissal of his report by his superiors surely did little to strengthen his confidence in authority. His disagreements with higher-ups would become exponentially worse in the course of the war into which his country had now been thrust.

In late 1942, Patton made a stop at Walter Reed Hospital before leaving for war. After months of deliberation, the Allied powers had decided on an invasion of North Africa. Patton would command the westernmost landings. On this day, however, the general was once again a young officer. Like Julius Caesar beseeching Jupiter himself for his blessing, Patton knelt before 81-year-old Gen. John "Black Jack" Pershing and asked his blessing in the war to come, which the visibly emotional general gave. On October 24, 1942, aboard the flagship *Augusta*, Patton left America to fulfill a destiny he had believed in since he was young. As F. Scott Fitzgerald wrote in *The Great Gatsby*, "No amount of fire or freshness can challenge what a man will store up in his ghostly heart." Patton would face the fire to live out his own words: "Compared to war, all [other] human activities are futile, if you like war as I do." He wrote in his diary: "It seems that my whole life has been pointed to this moment. When this job is done, I presume I will be pointed to the next step in the ladder of destiny. If I do my duty, the rest will take care of itself."

Patton's Soul

George Patton was driven by an innate sense of duty, both to his family's great military tradition and to his country. While he was an incredibly demanding commander, he loved his soldiers, and he pushed himself just as hard as he pushed them. He hated to lose any men but recognized that he would lose fewer if he used tactics that centered on speed; the shorter the battle, the fewer casualties.

He loathed incompetence, but more than that, he detested cowardice. By one account, David Irving's *The War Between the Generals*, Patton would take his pulse during an enemy bombardment and would chastise himself if his heart rate quickened. Ironically, he despised cowardice largely because his greatest fear was to be a coward himself; as such, he demanded the same standard of bravery from his fellow soldiers.

While Patton's ambition and pride often brought him into conflict with his superiors, they were not solely rooted in himself.

Rather, he was proud of his family's heritage, and he sought to increase the glory of that legacy through his own ambition. His ambition turned him from a dyslexic boy, thought by some to have ADD, into a man of culture, well read in history and literature, a passionate poet with a profound (albeit unorthodox) Christian faith. After making a successful landing in Morocco, Patton wrote:

> It is my firm conviction that the great success attending
> the hazardous operations carried out on sea and on land
> by the Western Task Force could only have been possible
> through the intervention of Divine Providence manifested
> in many ways. Therefore, I should be pleased if, in so
> far as circumstances and conditions permit, our grateful
> thanks be expressed today in appropriate religious services.

Because of his intense love of his family, his country, and his fellow soldiers, Patton sought to create the best possible outcome. When pursuing that outcome, however, he was often blunt and offensive to his superiors, especially if he thought they were sacrificing military practicality for political gain. He pushed others as hard as he pushed himself, no more, no less. That was the incarnation of George S. Patton; that was the soul of a warrior.

And now, with the United States at war, he had his greatest opportunity to bare that soul to the world—to grab hold of his destiny and show what it meant to be a man of war.

....

CHAPTER TWO

Man Up!

With America's entry into World War II, Patton's life was changed, and his destiny as a hard-charging military commander was secured. It is during the campaigns in North Africa and Italy that Patton's intrinsic sense of duty, honor, and loyalty unfolds. Here he demonstrates a fierce commitment to the men he leads, infusing them with the same purpose, courage, and determination that earned him the moniker "Old Blood and Guts."

Patton is the hardscrabble hero the Allies needed to break through the Axis strongholds, a leader undeterred by the gore and carnage of the battlefield. Of the soldiers who shared the grit and valor he esteemed and who would adhere to his discipline, Patton was demonstrably approving and sympathetic. As he learned from Gibbon in his *Decline and Fall of the Roman Empire*, though valor might be more present in some more than others, "such patient diligence can be the fruit only of habit and discipline." His success would begin with the very art of manliness (making boys into men), one disciplinary action at a time. Eat on time, dress like a soldier, before you declare yourself fit for battle. Honor yourself, and if not, honor the corp.

For those who fell short of his expectations, however, Patton was especially cruel. To many observers, Patton's treatment of his men was beyond harsh and callous—it was brutal, inappropriate, and indecorous. But dating back to his earliest days, it was Patton's own emotional vulnerability that he most feared would come out at times of weakness. So he knew what kept even the weakest of soldiers in check, if not for their lack of will. He understood from Machiavelli's *The Prince*, "It is much safer to be feared than loved because . . . love is preserved by the link of obligation which, owing to the baseness of men, is broken at every opportunity for their advantage; but fear preserves you by a dread of punishment which never fails." Gibbon would add, "and it was an inflexible maxim of Roman discipline, that a good soldier should dread his officers far more than the enemy."

As the drama in North Africa and Italy progressed, Patton presented a quandary for senior command: How much was too much? The theme would follow Patton throughout the war.

Playing in the Sand

Although Germany declared war on the United States mere days after the Pearl Harbor attack, and despite the fact that the United States and Great Britain had agreed to focus first on the European theater of operations, significant military action against Germany and Italy was delayed until almost a year later. Indeed, when Anglo-American forces launched Operation Torch in early November 1942, it was in North Africa, as the Allies sought to dislodge the vaunted German Afrika Korps and its relatively unimposing Italian counterparts. The Afrika Korps was commanded by Field Marshal Erwin Rommel, who was called the "Desert Fox" because of his reputation as a first-tier tank commander in the wasteland of North Africa.

Why North Africa? As naval historian Vincent P. O'Hara writes in *Torch*:

The military conundrum that faced the Anglo-American alliance in early 1942 was that Germany's smashing victory over France and the United Kingdom in June 1940 had denied the Allies a continental foothold. Thus, the road to victory would begin on a beach. There was no other choice.

Indeed, the Allies, under pressure from a beleaguered Stalin, knew they needed to take action if they wanted to avoid losing their Soviet allies. Because they lacked the strength to mount a campaign in Europe, they were forced to invade North Africa.

Operation Torch, viewed by planners as a massive risk, was led by U.S. Gen. Dwight D. Eisenhower, who exercised control over a byzantine command structure made up of both British and American officers. Although technically a joint Anglo-American operation, Torch was intended to have "a completely American complexion." The thinking was that the French in northwest Africa would be less resistant to an American invasion than a British one, as Anglo-French relations had drastically deteriorated.

Patton was placed in command of the Western Task Force and ordered to take the Moroccan capital of Casablanca. Patton's appointment was largely due to his knowledge of French culture and language, as well as his aristocratic upbringing. After being briefed on the operation in London, Patton returned to the United States, where he became "embroiled in such a distressing argument with the Navy Department that" he might have been relieved of his command, were it not for the intervention of his friend, Gen. Eisenhower, who knew "that the difficulty . . . was nothing more than the result of a bit of George's flair for the dramatic."

The Western Task Force had little trouble taking Casablanca, which surrendered within days of the initial Torch landings. In reflecting on the victory, Patton credited his men for their bravery, encouraging them to remember that "each one of you, is a representative of a great and victorious army. To be respected, you must inspire respect. . . . Your deeds have proven that you are fine soldiers. Look the part." He also issued an order that in recognition of "the intervention of Divine Providence manifested in many ways . . . our grateful thanks be expressed today in appropriate religious services."

For the time being, Patton had to remain behind the front lines, helping his rival and foil, the incredibly cautious Gen. Mark Clark, host the Casablanca Conference between Churchill and Roosevelt in January 1943. Because the rest of his responsibilities bored him, Patton would often travel to the front in Tunisia, both to study German and Italian operations (and why they were besting American tanks) and to get closer to the action. During this period, Patton became increasingly disillusioned with his superiors, as he viewed Eisenhower and Clark with rapidly decreasing respect for their indecisive natures. He was enraged by the decision, reached during the Casablanca Conference, to place British generals in command of American forces in North Africa, angrily exclaiming that "We have sold our birthright." Patton was especially irritated by the subordination of American men and officers to British command because of his virulent anglophobia.

While Patton waited anxiously for his chance to rejoin the fight, the Allies closed in on the German and Italian forces in Tunisia. Two weeks before the Torch landings, British Lt. Gen. Bernard Montgomery's Eighth Army engaged Axis forces in western Egypt, in what became known as the Second Battle of El Alamein. The Eighth Army's breakout just days before the beginning of Operation Torch forced Rommel to engage in a fighting retreat through Egypt and Libya back to Tunisia, joining up with the Axis forces defeated during Torch. Because the Allies failed to win the "Run for Tunis" (November–December 1942), in which they raced to reach Tunis before Axis reinforcements arrived, the Germans and Italians had been able to consolidate their position. Rommel's forces reached eastern Tunisia in mid-February and launched a devastating counterattack against U.S. II Corps, which had been advancing from the west, at the Battle of Kasserine Pass (February 19–24). The Axis armies consolidated their position at the Mareth Line, a defense system near the Libya-Tunisia border, constructed by the French prior to the war, reinforcing it with anti-aircraft and anti-tank guns, strengthened bunkers, over 60 miles of barbed wire, and almost 200,000 antitank and antipersonnel mines.

Following the crushing defeat at Kasserine Pass, Patton replaced disgraced Gen. Lloyd Fredendall as commander of II Corps. When ordered to report for active duty, it was clear that Patton's anglophobia was there to stay, as he confided to his diary: "I think I will have more trouble with the British than with the Boches [i.e., Germans]." Eisenhower warned Patton against causing trouble with their British allies, cautioning him to remember that his primary purpose was to attack the Italian First Army's rear, thereby assisting British Gen. Sir Harold Alexander in achieving a breakthrough. After an abortive spoiling attack on the advancing Eighth Army, Operation Capri, at Medenine on March 6, Axis forces found themselves in the undesirable position of having to defend the Mareth Line against Allied forces encroaching from the east and west.

As Patton made his way to Tunisia, he hoped he would be able to square off, one-on-one, in a tank joust against Gen. Erwin Rommel. Unbeknownst to Patton, Rommel had been replaced by Col. Gen. Hans-Jürgen von Arnim as commander-in-chief of the Heeresgruppe Afrika, or Army Group Africa, around the time that Patton took over II Corps. Rommel, meanwhile, flew back to Germany to receive treatment for a heart condition.

Patton arrived at II Corps headquarters on March 6, relieving Fredendall of his command. When he inherited II Corps, its men were disheveled, undisciplined, and demoralized. Knowing that he could not hope to defeat the Axis in North Africa without a well-disciplined force, Patton spent 10 days tightening regulations regarding attire, military courtesy, and punctuality and heightening the men's sense of hatred for the enemy. He required all personnel to wear helmets and insisted that all men wear neckties, at the risk of being fined or court-martialed (the idea being that a soldier who could not tie his tie and show up on time for breakfast would *not* properly handle a gun in war).

In addition to these superficial requirements, he instilled a fighting spirit in his men. Once, to express his disdain for the practice of digging in, Patton urinated in an old friend's foxhole. Of course, his vulgar, aggressive style did not sit well with all of his men, some of whom made a joke of his nickname, "Old Blood and Guts," reworking it as "our blood, his guts." Though he was tough on his men, Patton also worked to improve their quality of life, rushing clothing, mail, and equipment to them, in addition to demanding higher-quality food and cooking. In the midst of reforming II Corps into a legitimate fighting force, he was promoted to three-star general. While pleased with this development, as it fulfilled one of his lifelong dreams, Patton did not allow it to distract him from preparing his men for the coming fight.

On the eve of his offensive—his first as commanding officer—beginning with an attack on the town of Gafsa, Patton addressed the officers of II Corps, saying, "Gentlemen, tomorrow we attack. If we are not victorious, let no one come back alive." According to Omar Bradley, Patton then "excused himself and retired alone to his room to pray." Though Patton's words were "looked upon as a hammy gesture by his corps staff, it helped to make it more clearly apparent to them that to Patton war was a holy crusade."

In a rapid campaign, Patton's II Corps pushed the German and Italian forces eastward, as Montgomery's Eighth Army circumvented Axis defenses at the Mareth Line. This pincer movement culminated in an Axis surrender on May 13; the Allies had taken North Africa. Despite the successful coordination of British and American forces in driving the Axis from North Africa, Patton's abhorrence for the British only grew during the campaign. "God damn all British and all so-called Americans who have their legs pulled by them," he confided in his diary. "Ike is more British than the British and is putty in their hands."

Following the victory at Gafsa, Eisenhower replaced Patton as commander of II Corps, putting Gen. Omar Bradley in his place. The change allowed Patton to begin planning the upcoming invasion of Sicily.

Patton's ability to turn II Corps from a disheveled, demoralized group of inexperienced soldiers into a successful fighting force had revitalized the Allied war effort in North Africa, leading to an Anglo-American victory in that campaign. Unfortunately for Patton, he was unable to face Rommel, as Hitler prevented Rommel from returning to North Africa on account of his health.

Racing to Messina

Following his brilliant performance in North Africa, Patton helped plan the Allied invasion of Sicily, code-named Operation Husky (July 9–August 17, 1943). Fresh from their successful North African campaign, the Allies wanted to press their advantage. The Axis powers knew the Allies would invade Sicily but found themselves in the precarious position of never having defended against an invasion up to that point in the war; after all, it was the Vichy French, not the Germans or Italians, who engaged in an abortive defense against Torch. Furthermore, the action in North Africa had been of secondary importance to the German and Italian leadership, who considered it peripheral to the principal conflict in Europe. But now, the Allies prepared to attack the Axis on their own territory, in hopes of forcing an Italian surrender. If the fascist government of Benito Mussolini capitulated, the Germans would have to pick up the slack both in Italy and in the Balkans, lest they be exposed. This would draw more German men and material away from the Eastern Front, taking pressure off the Soviets and spreading the German military thin. Ultimately, opening a "second front" in Southern (and later Western) Europe proved to erode the Third Reich.

The decision to increase operations in the Mediterranean had been reached at the Casablanca Conference (January 14–25, 1943), though not without intense squabbling between the British and American military staffs. While the Americans favored a cross-Channel invasion of France (i.e., Operation Overlord) as the next Allied move, the British staff argued for the invasion of Sicily, along the lines of Churchill's desire to attack the "soft underbelly" of the Axis powers in Southern Europe. Ultimately, the British strategy won out; Overlord was pushed back, and planning for the invasion of Sicily continued apace. In a telegram to Stalin summarizing the results of the conference, Roosevelt and Churchill assured their Soviet counterpart, writing, "Our ruling purpose is to bring to bear upon Germany and Italy the maximum forces by land, sea and air which can be physically applied."

The Axis defense along the Sicilian coast was weak, allowing for a successful Allied landing. Despite the unreliability of their Italian allies, the Germans decided to mount a serious defense of the island. This strategy, conceived by German Oberbefehlshaber Süd (commander-in-chief in the south) and Generalfeldmarschall Albert Kesselring, aimed to delay both the fall of Sicily and the subsequent Allied invasion of Italy, in hopes of postponing the Italian surrender.

Placed in command of the Seventh Army, Patton distinguished himself throughout the course of the Sicilian campaign with his brilliant leadership and courage, often exposing himself to enemy fire while leading his men by example. He also distinguished himself in his conflicts with his superiors. Writing of Eisenhower's decision to place him under British commanding officers, Patton complained, "Ike has never been subjected to air attack or any other form of death. However, he is such a straw man that his future is secure. The British will never let him go." When British Field Marshal Harold Alexander ordered him to use the U.S. Seventh Army to cover the left flank of Montgomery's Eighth Army, Patton drove to Alexander's headquarters and protested, demanding instead that the Seventh Army be permitted to take the city of Palermo. Alexander granted the fiery American's request, and in a matter of days, one portion of the Seventh Army, under Gen. Geoffrey Keyes, had conducted a rapid advance and capture of that city, along with more than 50,000 German and Italian personnel.

A separate Seventh Army contingent under Gen. Omar Bradley had advanced to the northern coast of Sicily, thereby giving him a clear shot at capturing the city of Messina, as British Gen. Bernard Montgomery—one of Patton's many rivals—found himself bogged down near Catania. Messina was critically important to Allied operations, as it was the crucial port city on the Sicilian coast opposite the tip of the boot of Italy. Alexander's July 16 order that Montgomery's Eighth Army would capture Messina while Patton's Seventh Army engaged in mop-up operations enraged Patton. He accused "Monty" of "trying to steal the show, and with the assistance of Divine Destiny [Patton's sardonic nickname for Eisenhower] may do so," but took comfort in the fact that "to date we have captured three times as many men as our [British] cousins."

Patton knew he could and must take Messina before Montgomery as a matter of personal pride and for his men. He knew that the British looked down on the American soldiers as inexperienced and ineffective, and he wanted to prove them wrong.

He understood that in the ancient world, Messina had been the crown jewel of the Mediterranean and that it would be the key to the Allied invasion of Italy. As he wrote to Gen. Troy H. Middleton, "This is a horse race, in which the prestige of the U.S. Army is at stake. We must take Messina before the British." Further fueling Patton's already blazing desire to prove that his men could fight more effectively than the British was an erroneous story of the British Broadcasting Corporation (BBC), reporting that the British, not the Americans, had captured the city of Enna. The report further claimed that "the Seventh Army had been lucky to be in western Sicily eating grapes." Patton wanted to beat Montgomery to Messina so badly that he allegedly once told Bradley to "get into Messina just as fast as you can. I don't want you to waste time on these maneuvers even if you've got to spend men to do it. I want to beat Monty into Messina." Fortunately, Alexander ordered Patton to move toward Messina on July 23. Two days later, Hitler ordered the evacuation of all German formations from the island. His decision was prompted by the news that the Fascist Grand Council in Italy had stripped Mussolini of his power. "Thus," writes historian Harry Yeide, "it was Italian politics and the threat they posed to the lines of communication, and not Allied military pressure, that persuaded Hitler to order the evacuation of the island."

Patton's efforts were slowed by the withdrawal tactics of the Germans and Italians, who executed a fighting retreat from the island. In an attempt to cut them off, Patton ordered a series of amphibious landings behind the receding Axis line. Though the first, on August 8, failed to delay the Axis withdrawal, the second, on August 11, succeeded, despite the efforts of several Army and Navy officers to dissuade Patton of the operation's necessity. The August 11 operation forced the Germans and Italians to accelerate their withdrawal, which they executed brilliantly.

A third landing, on August 16, also opposed by Patton's subordinates, proved unnecessary, as the Third Division had already entered Messina, which had been abandoned by the Germans and the Italians. The city was officially surrendered to the Americans on the morning of August 17. Montgomery, whose forces had arrived too late, offered his compliments to Patton, saying, "It was a jolly good race. I congratulate you." The Sicily Campaign had been a huge success, with the Seventh Army capturing several critical cities and more than 100,000 German and Italian soldiers in the process. Filled with pride for his troops, Patton issued his famous General Order No. 18, which began: "Soldiers of the Seventh Army: Born at sea, baptized in blood, and crowned with victory, in the course of thirty-eight days of incessant battle and unceasing labor, you have added a glorious chapter to the history of war." He knew that because of their blood, sweat, and tears, he was finally beginning to fulfill his destiny as a great military leader.

A Slap in the Face

Patton's achievements on the battlefield were undermined, however, by his own bold and, at times, explosive nature. On July 15, Patton learned that after taking an airfield at Biscari, some of his men

> had taken my injunction to kill men who kept on shooting until we got within 200 yards, seriously, and had shot some 50 prisoners in cold blood and also in ranks, which was an even greater error. . . .[It] was probably an exaggeration, . . . [we should] certify that the dead men were snipers or had attempted to escape or something, as it would make a stink in the press and would also make the civilians mad.

Patton had delivered his "injunction" in two addresses he gave to officers on June 27, during which he seemingly directed them to kill all of the enemy. While interpretations of his order varied, he was certainly unclear in his delivery, and many interpreted his statement to mean that no quarter should be given, even to those German and Italian soldiers who had surrendered. It was not the first time Patton had encouraged war crimes against the enemy. According to Lindsey Nelson, who served under Patton and later became a well-known New York Mets broadcaster, Patton had once given a speech at Fort Bragg, North Carolina, in which he said of the Germans, "We'll rape their women and pillage their towns and run the pusillanimous sons-of-bitches into the sea." It seems this ultraviolent language was Patton's way of inspiring his men; Gen. Edwin Randle, who had also heard Patton's speech at Fort Bragg, noted, "At the end every man cheered, a genuine, spontaneous cheer. And there were cries of 'More! More!' Never before had they heard a general talk like that. He made a deep impression."

Another massacre of Axis prisoners of war, this time 36 in number, occurred in the wake of the capture of Biscari. In both cases, part of the explanation for the killings went back to Patton's ambiguous instructions regarding treatment of the enemy, to which a number of officers testified. Several other reports of shootings made their way back to Patton, who ordered that the massacres stop. Reluctantly, Patton ordered that the commanding officers in the two Biscari massacres be court-martialed. One was given a life sentence—he was freed after a year—and the other was found not guilty but was later killed in action, ironically while going forward alone to investigate a white flag raised by the Germans. Several months later, a government investigation found that Patton was responsible for the massacres, given the content of his speeches, but did not recommend that any action be taken against him, and so none was. It seems that, at best, Patton's orders were unclear; at worst, he may have actually given an order that no Axis soldiers be given quarter.

About a week after learning of the Biscari shootings, Patton encountered a local farmer whose mules were blocking a narrow bridge, thereby preventing the passage of his troops. Patton, enraged, shot each of the mules through the head and had them thrown off the bridge. He then beat the driver with his walking stick, breaking it in the process. When recounting the episode in a letter to Beatrice several months later, he wrote, "Human rights are being exalted over our victory." Though brutal, this episode reflected Patton's realization that if his column of men was stalled at the bridge, they would make an easy target for the Luftwaffe. He had to make a quick decision about what to do, as their Stuka dive-bombers could have swept down at any moment and decimated his soldiers.

The incident with the mules speaks to Patton's discord with the prevailing sensibilities of the era's progressives, a tension that military historian Victor Davis Hanson attributes to the phenomenon of therapeutic societies. Hanson explains:

> Democracies are therapeutic societies and we don't train
> people, thank God, to kill people. But there are people in
> the world who do [kill people] and when they do, they
> need people like George Patton, who understand the evil
> mind and can make soldiers for brief periods of time who
> can have the training, and the courage, and the fortitude
> to stand up to [the enemy].

The worst blow to Patton's reputation was yet to come, however. More than any other event, Patton's victories in North Africa and Italy were overshadowed by his controversial treatment of two soldiers in early August 1943. In separate incidents, both in the wake of his exhausting three-week campaign in Sicily, Patton slapped two soldiers, who were each recovering from combat fatigue (previously known as shell shock) in evacuation hospitals, accusing both of cowardice.

More than other officers, Patton frequently visited wounded soldiers in the hospital. It was a way to connect with his men— although an unusual practice for a senior officer—and revealed a genuinely compassionate side of the hardened general. Patton was often moved by the heroism and sacrifice of the young fighters, and the visits came to be deeply emotional. After one such visit following a particularly brutal series of losses in the field, he wrote in his diary: "One man had the top of his head blown off and they were just waiting for him to die. He was a horrid bloody mess and was not good to look at, or I might develop personal feelings about sending men to battle. That would be fatal for a General."

Thus, when Patton encountered the two soldiers he viewed as cowards taking up space in hospital beds, he made his wrath felt. Of one of the incidents, Patton wrote that a soldier was "trying to look as if he had been wounded. I asked him what was the matter, and he said he just couldn't take it. I gave him the devil, slapped his face with my gloves and kicked him out of the hospital. Companies should deal with such men, and if they shirk their duty they should be tried for cowardice and shot." To the hospital commander, Patton said, "I can't help it, but it makes my blood boil to think of a yellow bastard being babied. I won't have those cowardly bastards hanging around our hospitals. We'll probably have to shoot them some time anyway, or we'll raise a breed of morons." Only those who knew Patton well understood how emotionally charged he was around his brave, wounded boys.

Initially, Eisenhower managed to keep the slapping incidents out of the press, as he did not want to court-martial Patton. Writing about the incident years after the fact, Ike mused that "Patton's offense, had it been committed on the actual front, would not have been an offense. It would merely have been an incident of battle—no one would have even noted it, except with the passing thought that here was a leader who would not tolerate shirking." The Supreme Allied Commander wrote an emotional letter to Patton on August 17—the same day the Seventh Army took Messina—to which he attached the official report of Patton's misdeeds. Though Eisenhower sympathized with Patton, saying, "I am well aware of the necessity for hardness and toughness on the battlefield," he refused to "excuse brutality, abuse of the sick, nor exhibition of uncontrollable temper in front of subordinates."

Frustrated, Ike told Patton, "I must so seriously question your good judgment and your self-discipline as to raise serious doubts in my mind as to your future usefulness." He concluded on a personal note, writing, "No letter that I have been called upon to write in my military career has caused me the mental anguish of this one," citing his "warm and deep personal friendship for you" and his "admiration for your military qualities" but reminding Patton that such actions could not and would "not be tolerated in this theater no matter who the offender may be."

As a result of his error, Patton was not permitted to participate in the Italian campaign. It was hardly the last time he would be punished for making his superiors look bad. Instead, he served to distract the Germans, as he was moved around the Mediterranean from place to place in such a way as to distract their attention. Allied officials assumed that the Germans paid close attention to Patton's movements because they considered him to be the Allies' most skilled fighting general, and so his travel between North Africa, Palestine (specifically Jerusalem), Egypt, Malta, and elsewhere distracted them. They also assumed that the Germans feared his transferral to a new location meant an attack was imminent, not least because they could not believe that the Americans would keep their best general out of the battle merely for slapping some soldiers. Speculation as to his location raged in the presses, with some rumors even alleging that he was in India or Burma. Historian Harry Yeide wrote that, in reality,

> [t]here does not appear to be an iota of fact behind this claim. The notion that Patton could be used to deceive the Germans appears to have arisen from a presumption about German thinking in Washington rather than any evidence that the Germans had a particular interest in the general's activities.

Yeide wrote that the reasoning behind American strategists' assumption was simple:

> the United States had no other seasoned and widely known general other than Eisenhower. . . . From the German perspective, Patton was simply one blip in a noisy pattern of very dangerous enemy commanders, many of whom . . . probably loomed much larger than Patton in their thinking.

Most historians would think otherwise, including Eisenhower and Patton himself, as we will see.

In September, Patton was crushed to learn that Bradley had been appointed to command the First Army in the upcoming Normandy invasion. He had hoped that command of the First Army would fall to him so that he could finally return to the battlefield and continue his pursuit of military glory.

Ike was able to protect Patton from the reporters who wished to relate these events to the American public; after all, he needed Patton's fighting mind and spirit. In fact, he did not even have to pressure the dozens of British and American reporters in Sicily and Algiers to keep the story under wraps. But by November 1943, an NBC radio correspondent leaked the story to popular columnist Drew Pearson, a rumormonger with a reputation for using scandal to destroy his political opponents. He broke the story on November 21, sullying Patton's character and questioning his ability to command, despite the fact that he was the winningest general in the Army.

Now his character was called into question, along with his ability to command. According to Victor Davis Hanson, "Rumors abounded that Patton was unhinged, that he might have shot somebody." He continues that it became "[a] cause to celebrate that we have an out of control General." Jonathan Jordan, author of *Brothers, Rivals, Victors: Eisenhower, Patton, Bradley and the Partnership That Drove the Allied Conquest in Europe*, adds, "Patton's uproar was a court-martialing offense. Officers could not strike enlisted men."

All the worse for Patton, journalist Pearson leveled criticism against Eisenhower as well, for having failed to issue an official reprimand, though, in reality, Eisenhower had privately rebuked Patton for his actions.

The story came to define Pearson as an opportunistic wartime journalist who was more than happy to expose the proverbial skeletons in others' closets for his own gain. Even FDR had strong words for this muckraker: "His ill-considered falsehoods have come to the point where he is doing much harm to his own Government and to other nations. It is a pity that anyone anywhere believes anything he writes." Though other war correspondents kept the slapping incidents quiet for fear that the story might damage morale, provide fuel for German propaganda, or possibly even reduce Patton's effectiveness in future combat assignments. Pearson exaggerated them. He falsely reported that the private in question was visibly "out of his head," telling Patton to "duck down or the shells would hit him," and that in response, "Patton struck the soldier, knocking him down." Pearson punctuated his broadcast by twice stating that Patton would never again be used in combat, despite the fact that Pearson had no factual basis for this prediction.

More than a century before, Napoleon also had contended with the press:

> Instead of all the stupidness with which the daily press is filled, why do you not send commissioners to visit the districts from which we have expelled the enemy and make them collect the details of the crimes that have been committed there? Nothing more powerful could be found to stir the minds than a recital of the details. What we need at this moment is real and serious things, not wit in prose and verse. My hair stands on end when I hear of the crimes committed by the enemy, and the police have not even thought of obtaining a single account of these happenings. . . . A picture drawn in larger strokes will not convince the people. With ink and paper, you can draw any pictures you like. Only by telling the facts simply and with detail can we convince them.

Pearson broke the story in his evening broadcast on Sunday, November 21, 1943, having cleared it with the Office of Censorship and the War Department. He added fuel to the fire by noting that the first soldier Patton slapped was Jewish, thereby implying that Patton was antisemitic.

Indeed, according to journalists who witnessed the aftermath of the second slapping, Patton asserted that combat fatigue was simply "an invention of the Jews," which certainly did not help matters any. Besides revealing a possible—though not uncommon—antisemitism in Patton's mind, this remark also demonstrates Patton's firm belief that combat fatigue was a made-up condition and that those who suffered from it were simply cowards who needed to be angered so as to regain their fighting spirit. While, of course, Patton was wrong in that combat fatigue, post-traumatic stress disorder, and other psychological conditions often result from combat, it is important to understand this belief in the broader context of his extreme disdain for cowardice, real or perceived (and that many fighting generals might have questioned the diagnosis at the time).

To the medical officer who accompanied Patton, it seemed an almost commonplace experience at the time. As author Blumeson recounts:

> The shells going over him bothered him. The next day he was worried about his buddy and became more nervous. He was sent down to the rear echelon by a battery aid man and there the medical aid man gave him some medicine which made him sleep, but still he was nervous and disturbed. On the next day the medical officer ordered him to be evacuated, although the boy begged not to be evacuated because he did not want to leave his unit.

Ironically, it seems that part of the explanation for Patton's intransigence lies in the fact that he was likely suffering from combat fatigue himself. He was most certainly worn down, having obsessed over beating the British, under Montgomery, to Messina. Patton was mercurial, a fact that may be explained by the numerous head injuries he suffered throughout his life. As Blumenson hypothesizes, the number of blows Patton suffered to his head "may have eventually produced a permanent condition, perhaps a subdural hematoma, a pool of blood around his brain. This condition could sometimes have made it difficult for Patton to stifle his aggressions and his emotions, his temper as well as his tears." While Blumenson's suggestion that Patton's history of head injuries affected his emotions has some merit, the notion that Patton could have lived that long with a subdural hematoma without experiencing other symptoms (besides those affecting his emotions) seems far-fetched. Some of his emotional instability, however, could very well have come from brain trauma or from an undiagnosed mental condition.

Regardless of the possibilities of Patton's own mental or physical state, one this is certain: he would not abide cowardice. According to his daughter, Ruth Ellen, as quoted in George Forty's book, *Patton's Third Army at War*, Patton "hated to see men killed. . . . [H]e felt a coward has less of a chance to stay alive, because fear dulls intuition, and cowardice is catching—the Greeks called it panic." Alexander the Great, too, acknowledged the battle of fear as part of the human condition, saying: "Through every generation of the human race there has been a constant war, a war with fear. Those who have the courage to conquer it are made free and those who are conquered by it are made to suffer until they have the courage to defeat it, or death takes them." It is clear that the reasons behind Patton's actions were multifarious and that, in a sense, he was doing what he thought was best for his men.

In the final assessment, then, Patton's infamous slapping incidents, though appalling, should be viewed as more than simply the actions of a cruel man of war. Rather, Patton acted out of a mixture of personal belief, stress, and emotion.

Even so, despite his heroic efforts to secure Sicily for the Allies, Patton was sidelined. The opposing armies would ahve found the whole episode absurd. Victor Davis Hanson speaks to this point, saying: "No one could believe you would dismiss your top ranking soldier because he slapped somebody. They all felt that the only good commander the Americans had so far fielded by 1944 was Patton."

By comparison, the disciplinary actions of our supposed Soviet allies would have been judged nothing short of atrocities. In the case of Stalin's attack on Polish leadership in the Katyn Forest, the act was pure genocide. Toward the end of the war, it was the Nazis themselves who most keenly understood the Soviets' policy on prisoners and civilians, even in postwar occupation. It was why they so desperately surrendered to the Americans when possible. In retrospect, we are aware of the Soviets' track record, and it would require a book of its own to unpack. But in comparison to the Soviet level of tragedy, could a simple slap have been anything but a trivial misstep? Or at least worthy of privacy until the war was over?

According to the studies, 107 senior officers, including a marshal, 72 generals, 6 admirals and commanders of divisions and heads of political staffs were arrested during those 12 months. Forty-five of these were sentenced to be shot, including 34 generals. Ten more died while under arrest.

Patton's opponents were baffled.

Ultimately, Patton was spared a court-martial, as Eisenhower opted instead to have him apologize both to the men he had slapped and to their respective units. He did so reluctantly, insisting that his reasoning was still sound. When apologizing to the witnesses of the slappings, including soldiers, doctors, and nurses, he "told them about my friend in the last war [World War I] who shirked, was let get by with it, and eventually killed himself. I told them that I had taken the action I had, to correct such a future tragedy." Indeed, this reflected the logic that apparently drove him in both instances; after slapping the second soldier, he confided to his diary, "I may have saved his soul if he had one." When he personally apologized to both men, they seemed to harbor no ill will toward their commander.

Beatrice Patton would write:

> He had been known to weep at men's graves—as well as tear their hides off. The deed is done and the mistake made, and I'm sure Georgie is sorrier and has punished himself more than anyone could possibly realize. I've known George Patton for 31 years and I've never known him to be deliberately unfair. He's made mistakes—and he's paid for them. This was a big mistake, and he's paying a big price for it.

Relegated to England as Overlord advanced, Patton, in a very real sense, became a casualty of war, just as if he had suffered a disabling physical wound. Patton paid a high price for his actions, but the cost to Patton is known: 11 months on the sidelines. The cost to the Allied war effort can only be guessed. Historian Victor Davis Hanson notes that "there's a pattern here of somebody who has undeniable experience, preparation and natural genius, who understands the horrific nature of war. And yet, time and time again when he is not given a promotion befitting what he has earned on the battlefield, people die."

For Patton, sitting out the Normandy invasion was unbearable. The long-carried vision of himself leading a great army on the world stage had been forcibly postponed as he watched Montgomery and Bradley make history. His destiny was in the balance and depended on a chance to join the Allies, even as Ike's call to arms reverberated across armed forces radios:

> Soldiers, sailors and airmen of the Allied Expeditionary forces, you are about to embark on the Great Crusade.

The eyes of the world are upon you. The hopes and prayers of liberty loving people everywhere march with you.

You will bring about the destruction of the German war machine, the elimination of Nazi tyranny over the oppressed people of Europe and security for ourselves in a free world.

As Patton watched the war unfold, he uncharacteristically offered quiet and tempered support of his superiors in an attempt to regain their trust. He writes in his diary:

Ike broadcast to occupied Europe and did it well. None of the troops of this army are in yet and in fact I doubt if the enemy knows of its existence. We will try to give him quite a surprise. . . . I can't tell when I will go in. . . . However I have had my bag packed for some time just in case. It is Hell to be on the side lines and see all the glory eluding me, but I guess there will be enough for all. . . . I guess I will read the Bible.

Victor Davis Hanson notes that a tragic consequence of the slapping incident was America's seeming loss—both romantically and practically—of its greatest and most galvanizing hero of the day. In effect, General Eisenhower put Patton on ice in Sicily. That decision was detrimental to the success of the Italian campaign, notes Hanson: "We know that from the fall of 1943 all the way to May of 1945, we never took Italy. We lost over 80,000 dead, but we never got up the Alps. A lot of people got killed in Italy . . . that otherwise probably wouldn't have had to die." The calculus may have been far different had Patton been available as the supreme commander in the theater.

······································

CHAPTER THREE

On the Sidelines

The decision to remove Patton from command in Italy and sideline him at precisely the moment the Allies were gearing up for their major offensive would prove costly. Patton knew it before senior command did. Yet he was blind to his own flaws and unwilling to temper his own instincts even when doing so might have changed the course of the war and his legacy. The ancients would have characterized this defect as *hubris*.

Pressured by a democratic press and a prevailing sense of propriety that placed a premium on decorum, Eisenhower had no choice but to sideline Patton after the slapping incident in Italy. Patton's behavior there had not aligned with the political correctness of the era; never mind that he had been victorious. In the role of antihero, Patton was a perfect foil for the tension created between virtue and imperfection.

By his own admission, Patton was distraught: "It is very heartbreaking. The only time I have felt worse was the night of December 9th, 1942, when Clark got the Fifth Army. . . . I feel like death but will survive—I always have."

In Exile

While Patton was sidelined by Eisenhower and denied a direct role in the Normandy invasion, some of the most crucial military and diplomatic events of the war took place, fundamentally shaping the postwar world. As the fighting heated up, so did the politics. In November and December 1943, Roosevelt, Churchill, and Stalin met to decide the strategy of the war at a conference in Tehran, Iran. The Big Three, largely pressured by Stalin to distract the Germans from the fighting on the Eastern front, committed to opening a second front against Nazi Germany in May 1944; this action was delayed until June of that year. Stalin, a master of geopolitical chess, played down the importance of Berlin, though he had every intention of taking the jewel of Europe and, rather than liberating the German people from the Nazis, capturing them for communism. Patton was aware of this. Stalin knew that he was in a losing race with the United States to build an atomic bomb and that Berlin held the Nazis' atomic secrets.

Churchill, however, even as early as 1943, had begun to see a new threat to Europe—the man who had become the third ally in the fight against Hitler, Josef Stalin. He told Anthony Eden, "It would be a measureless disaster if Russian barbarism overlaid the ancient states of Europe." Despite Churchill's best efforts to force the primary Allied invasion through southern Italy, Stalin and Roosevelt insisted on a cross-channel invasion of western France, Operation Overlord, coupled with an invasion of France's southern coast, and refused to divert men and material from that effort to support Mediterranean operations. This decision greatly frustrated Churchill, as he saw operations in the Mediterranean as essential to preventing the spread of communism in that region after the war.

Despite the decision to focus Western efforts on the Overlord landings, Anglo-American operations still continued in the Mediterranean, as they sought to push up the Italian peninsula and into German territory. Since the fascist government of Italy, under Benito Mussolini, had surrendered to the Allies in September 1943, the remaining Axis troops in Italy were predominantly German.

After reaching a stalemate in the Liri Valley, in the shadow of Monte Cassino, Gen. Mark Clark—who had replaced Patton as commander of the Fifth Army—decided to conduct an amphibious assault at the town of Anzio in hopes of outflanking the Germans and then crushing them in a pincer movement. The assault began on January 22, 1944, but stalled due to overall incompetence throughout the ranks. This allowed the Germans to launch a brutal counterattack on the Allied beachhead in February. Due to the poor, indecisive leadership of Clark and others, the Allies sustained tens of thousands of casualties. Had Patton been allowed to command the Fifth Army at Anzio, it is probable that thousands of British and American soldiers could have been spared, since Patton would have pushed past the beachhead as quickly as possible, rather than waiting for more support as Clark and his officers had done.

On the day of the Anzio landings, Patton was recalled to England. After that operation failed, Eisenhower considered putting Patton back into action under Clark but ultimately decided to keep him in England. The eventual taking of Rome would be an extended and brutal affair and cost much blood and treasure. Instead of Patton, Eisenhower decided to promote Gen. Lucian Truscott, Jr., who was already with Clark in Italy. The debacle at Anzio was a drain on supplies, postponing the invasion of France. Originally, Anglo-American military planners scheduled a May 1944 launch of Operation Overlord, but the date was ultimately moved to June 6.

Training and Trickery

Patton knew he must come to terms with the fact that he would not be seeing action for the opening of the largest invasion in history. Viewing the Normandy shores must have triggered memories of the Great Trojan War, American Revolution, Gallipoli—epic, legendary events he had played over and over in his mind for decades. The only difference was, during this reincarnation, he was not on the battlefield. He appears to have shifted his value from battlefield commander to the world's best decoy, as he longed for the day he would reemerge, now with the added element of deception and surprise.

Patton knew that Revolutionary War Gen. George Washington also used secrecy and deception to his advantage to defend against the larger, better equipped, and better trained British regular army and its Hessian mercenaries. It was Washington's decision to hire a spy that would allow colonial forces to find the Hessian camp and strike on Christmas Eve 1776. The secret maneuver would trigger a series of victories in Trenton and Princeton that would also turn the tide of the war. Patton also embraced the words of Macchiavelli, in his discourses on Livy:

> Never attempt to win by force what can be won by deception. Although to use deception in any action is detestable, nevertheless in waging war it is praiseworthy and brings fame: he who conquers the enemy by deception is praised as much as he who conquers them by force.

Luckily for Patton, shortly after arriving in England, he was secretly assigned to train the inexperienced U.S. Third Army, preparing them for action in Europe following the Overlord landings. He took to his task with great enthusiasm, reflective of his love for training and discipline. He visited the various units within the Third Army, riling up the enlisted men with vulgar and provocative addresses and instructing the officers calmly, quietly, and meticulously. He stressed the importance of discipline and order, especially in how his men presented themselves. Patton complained that the men of the Third Army were "willing to die but not anxious to kill. I tell them that it is fine to be willing to die for their country but a damned sight better to make the German die for his."

He instilled confidence in his men, saying:

I can assure you that the Third United States Army will be the greatest army in American history. We shall be in Berlin ahead of everyone. To gain that end, we must have perfect discipline. I shall drive you until hell won't have it. . . . We are going to kill German bastards—I would prefer to skin them alive—but, gentlemen, I fear some of our people at home would accuse me of being too rough.

As recounted by Blumenson, one soldier under Patton's command said that his speeches made one feel "as if you had been given a supercharge from some divine source. Here was the man for whom you would go to hell and back."

If we deconstruct Patton's speech to his men, we see a series of themes that were with him from his first chance at war and now were coming to fruition in his greatest moment. He began with a reminder of American greatness, historically demonstrated by its comfort with competition:

When you, here, every one of you, were kids, you all admired the champion marble player, the fastest runner, the toughest boxer, the big league ball players, and the All-American football players. Americans love a winner.

Americans will not tolerate a loser. Americans despise
cowards. Americans play to win all of the time. I wouldn't
give a hoot in hell for a man who lost and laughed. That's
why Americans have never lost nor will ever lose a war; for
the very idea of losing is hateful to an American.

He followed that sentiment with a reminder of the soldier's
honor and duty in light of his possible death:

Death must not be feared. Death, in time, comes to all
men. Yes, every man is scared in his first battle. If he says
he's not, he's a liar. Some men are cowards, but they fight
the same as the brave men or they get the hell slammed
out of them watching men fight who are just as scared as
they are. The real hero is the man who fights even though
he is scared. Some men get over their fright in a minute
under fire. For some, it takes an hour. For some, it takes
days. But a real man will never let his fear of death overpower his honor, his sense of duty to his country, and his
innate manhood.

Next, he addressed the significant role of the individual in the
context of the team: "Every single man in this Army plays a vital
role. Don't ever let up. Don't ever think that your job is unimportant. Every man has a job to do and he must do it. Every man is a
vital link in the great chain."

And then, a reminder that the soldier at the least risk is the one
in motion and leading the aggression, or blitzkrieg, he admonished
that holding, waiting, or opening long-stayed lines in war was high-
risk behavior due to the drain of supplies and loss of blood and
treasure:

I don't want to get any messages saying, "I am holding my position." We are not holding a goddamned thing. Let the Germans do that. We are advancing constantly and we are not interested in holding onto anything, except the enemy's balls. We are going to twist his balls and kick the living shit out of him all of the time. Our basic plan of operation is to advance and to keep on advancing regardless of whether we have to go over, under, or through the enemy.

Patton's words, though filled with characteristic vulgarity, clearly echoed one of his heroes, the great military theorist Clausewitz: "For political and social as well as for military reasons the preferred way of bringing about victory was the shortest, most direct way, and that meant using all possible force."

And, of course, Patton pulled no punches with his men but forced them to confront fear with the realist acceptance of the violent nature of war:

War is a bloody, killing business. You've got to spill their blood, or they will spill yours. Rip them up the belly. Shoot them in the guts. When shells are hitting all around you and you wipe the dirt off your face and realize that instead of dirt it's the blood and guts of what once was your best friend beside you, you'll know what to do!

Finally, Patton would conclude by calling his men to join him writing their collective destiny:

You may be thankful that twenty years from now when you are sitting by the fireplace with your grandson on your knee and he asks you what you did in the great

World War II, you WON'T have to cough, shift him to
the other knee and say, "Well, your Granddaddy shoveled
shit in Louisiana." No, Sir, you can look him straight in
the eye and say, "Son, your Granddaddy rode with the
Great Third Army and a Son-of-a-Goddamned-Bitch
named Georgie Patton!"

An important aspect of Overlord was a cover plan—Operation
Fortitude—designed to mislead the Germans as to the true location of the imminent Allied invasion. Patton, still on the sidelines
in England, had been earmarked to serve as a decoy in Operation
Fortitude South, which was intended to make the Germans think
that the Allies would invade France at the Pas de Calais. (Its counterpart, Operation Fortitude North, aimed to trick them into
thinking that the Allies were planning to attack Norway from
Russia and Scotland.) If Patton could not lead the army on the
battlefield, he could serve as subterfuge to divert Rommel's troops
away from the Normandy beaches and toward Calais. He would
admonish his men:

> Remember, men, you don't know I'm here. No mention of
> that is to be made in any letters. The USA is supposed to
> be wondering what the Hell has happened to me. I'm not
> supposed to be commanding this Army, I'm not supposed
> even to be in England. Let the first bastards to find out be
> the Goddam Germans. I want them to look up and howl,
> "ACH, IT'S THE GODDAM THIRD ARMY AND
> THAT SON-OF-A-BITCH PATTON AGAIN!"

Calais was the closest part of France to England and housed
heavy German defenses. While Allied planners had decided not
to attack at Calais because of its strong fortification and troop

concentration, they wanted the Germans to think that they were attacking there, because it was the shortest distance across the English Channel, it was a hub for an extensive transportation network, and it was the primary launch site for German V-1 and V-2 rocket attacks on England.

Fortitude South relied upon several means to trick the Germans into thinking the invasion of France would come at Calais. These included double agents, disinformation, and the creation of the bogus and highly publicized First U.S. Army Group, or FUSAG, under General Patton. FUSAG was comprised of some real military units, but most of their formations were created using dummy landing craft, tanks, and the like to fool German aerial reconnaissance. The plan was so elaborate as to include bogus stories for the soldiers in each "unit"—for instance, fake wedding announcements in local newspapers—and patches for soldiers to wear, signifying the "ghost division" to which they belonged.

Using Patton, the general the Germans were thought to most fear and respect, as a decoy was perhaps the boldest stroke of the grand deception. American officials assumed that as German high command saw it, the invasion would come from where Patton was. Much of the historiography on Patton echoes this assumption. As Harry Yeide suggests, however, Patton played a negligible role in German thinking leading up to Operation Overlord. While true that the Germans had their own name for FUSAG—Armeegruppe Patton, or Army Group Patton—this designation (indicating that Patton was the ostensible commander of FUSAG) came about months after he was known to have been affiliated with FUSAG and, more important, months after the Germans had concluded that the Allies would likely invade at Pas de Calais or in Belgium. As such, "his fictional command of FUSAG did not contribute to that analysis." Furthermore, "Patton was only one small piece in the deception operation, a fact underscored by the continued German treatment of FUSAG as real and a potential threat even after Patton appeared at the head of the Third Army in Normandy."

Patton, too, was incredulous. He wrote in his diary: "It is Hell to be on the side lines and see all the glory eluding me, but I guess that there will be enough for all." Indeed, it was no small irony that the general had been suspended for the slappings while his duty was quite literally to send men into extremely dangerous combat situations in which they would likely die.

Eisenhower chose Gen. Omar Bradley over Patton to command the First Army in preparation for Operation Overlord, saying that "Bradley . . . is, in my opinion, the best rounded combat leader I have yet met in our service. While he possibly lacks some of the extraordinary and ruthless driving power that Patton can exert at critical moments . . . he is among our best."

A Close Call

Though the media openly discussed Patton's role as commander of the First Army Group, extreme care was taken to keep his whereabouts hidden from the Germans.

Shortly before the beginning of Operation Overlord, however, Patton's cover was nearly blown and the mission nearly exposed by a speech he gave to the Welcome Club for American GIs in Knutsford on the night of April 25. Eisenhower had explicitly warned him against making public statements and holding press conferences, saying, "He had a genius for explosive statements that rarely failed to startle his hearers. He had so long practiced the habit of attempting with fantastic pronouncements to astound his friends and associates that it had become second nature with him, regardless of circumstances."

In his speech at Knutsford, Patton clarified that his opening remarks were made on an unofficial basis. He made some brief comments, at one point asserting, "I believe with Mr. [George] Bernard Shaw, I think it was he, that the British and Americans are two separate people separated by a common language, and since it is the evident destiny of the British and the Americans, and, of course, the Russians to rule the world, the better we know each other, the better job we will do."

Having given his remarks, Patton left, politely declining an invitation to stay for dinner so as to avoid any confusion about his role there. Unfortunately, he later discovered that contrary to what he had been told, there had been a reporter at the event. Patton's remarks were soon splashed across British and American newspapers.

Once again, the press distorted his comments, doctoring them to make it appear that he had left out any mention of the Russians in the postwar order. He was castigated both for his supposed exclusion of the Russians and for comments he made regarding relations between American GIs and English ladies, in which he implied that the latter would make American women jealous and accelerate the end of the war in Europe. Such remarks—often misrepresented in a crasser way—were denounced as inappropriate for a man of his rank.

Thus, despite "really trying to be careful," Patton now found himself in yet another public relations mess. Eisenhower was livid, not least because he had warned Patton against making public statements. As Ike complained to Omar Bradley: "I'm just about fed up. If I have to apologize publicly for George once more, I'm going to have to let him go, valuable as he is. I'm getting sick and tired of having to protect him. Life's much too short to put up with any more of it." "For the first time," Eisenhower recalled, "I began seriously to doubt my ability to hang onto my old friend, in whose fighting capacity I had implicit faith and confidence." Ike was so angry that he seriously considered sending Patton home.

Patton himself was extremely frustrated with the turn of events, complaining that he had been misunderstood and that he had been told that no reporters would be present. He wrote in his diary: "None of those at Ike's headquarters ever go to bat for juniors, and in any argument between the British and the Americans, invariably favor the British. Benedict Arnold is a piker compared with them, and that includes [Gen. John C. H.] Lee as well as Ike and [Gen. Walter] Beedle [sic; Smith]."

Fortunately for Patton, however, circumstances prevented Eisenhower from firing him. The Supreme Allied Commander invited Patton to explain himself in a personal meeting on May 1, 1944. During that meeting, Eisenhower explained that "his hand was being forced in the United States" and that Patton had put him in a bad spot yet again. Patton left the meeting unsure of his fate, writing that he felt "like death, but I am not out yet. If they will let me fight, I will; but if not, I will resign so as to be able to talk, and then I will tell the truth and possibly do my country more good."

Upon investigating the matter, Eisenhower learned two critical pieces of information that swayed his judgment. First, he learned that "in advance of the meeting Patton had refused to make any speech and had merely, under the insistence of his hosts, risen to his feet to say a word or two in support of the purpose of the particular gathering." Second, Patton had made his remarks under the impression that they would not be reported. By May 4, Eisenhower cabled Patton, informing him that "I have decided to keep you. . . . Go ahead and train your Army."

General Marshall had given Eisenhower the authority to make the decision himself, advising him "not [to] weaken your hand for Overlord." Ike had concluded that he needed Patton, both for his ability as a fighting general and for his part in the Fortitude South deception operation, and he let Patton know he was retaining him "solely because of my faith in you as an able battle leader and from no other motives," thereby putting him on notice that he could not have any more slip-ups. In a meeting, Eisenhower jokingly told

Patton, "You owe us some victories; pay off and the world will deem me a wise man."

It was certainly for the best that Patton had not been sent home, for if that had been the case, the Germans would surely have paid far less attention to the location of the Third Army in England, and the Patton decoy would have thus failed. If Fortitude South had failed, that would have greatly imperiled the success of Operation Overlord, which commenced on June 6. Despite this, Patton had to wait almost a month before he would set foot on the Continent and engage the Germans once more in the waning months of World War II.

The voice that roared to urge American soldiers forward had been muzzled, and with it, a great embodiment of the American fighting spirit. By giving Patton a secondary role in the invasion, Eisenhower inadvertently slowed the progress of the war, as Bradley quickly became bogged down in the Norman bocage country with Operation Cobra, largely because of his cautious nature. Thus, as at Anzio, more American and British lives were lost because the campaign lacked the brash, driving style of Patton under General Clark. Once he was finally back on the battlefield and his muzzle had been removed, spectacular results followed.

With the passing of time, as American GIs jumped from amphibious boats onto the beaches of Normandy, greeted by a nonstop spray of machine gun fire from fortified Nazi pillboxes, Eisenhower and the remaining brass must have hearkened back to the moment they had asked the press not to publish the slapping incident. The morals, or even appropriate niceties, of peacetime might have been an overreach for this moment in Allied efforts. Should those mothers back in the States pay a price with the lives of their 19-year-old boys because of one impulsive general? Couldn't this high-risk venture have been filed temporarily under the, at times, amoral nature of war?

We will never know how Eisenhower would calibrate the costs of not having Patton on the front lines, but the fact was clear that Omar Bradley remained trapped on the Normandy beaches. Rommel had long planned for a landing, and his defense was strong. Patton, along with many others, had long respected Rommel, as his prowess came not from his skill alone but also from the fact that he was not part of the Nazi Party. To Patton, this showed Rommel to be an honorable man serving a dishonorable system. Patton did not know that even if he had been given the chance at the invasion, he still would not have faced his peer, as Rommel had returned home for his wife's birthday. By the time Rommel returned, his forces had been breached at many points on the front. Patton's red herring—his make-believe army invading at Calais—would prove to be merely a partial distraction.

In retrospect, Patton might have seemed, at times, tone deaf to the needs of his frightened or injured men, but he was not tone deaf about killing Nazis. Finally unleashed on the beach, Patton would run Operation Cobra 2 with coordinated air and ground attack and make necessary U.S. progress on the ground. The Third Army, under the hard-driving leadership of cavalryman Patton, had an open field. He would build an unstoppable momentum that would sweep across France.

Once on French soil, Patton would no longer have to sit on the sidelines of war with only his ghosts for company. Now he would be let loose to chase his destiny once again. He was not alone; he had his men, and he understood each one would play a vital role. Together they would make up an unstoppable army. From Patton's "Speech to the Third Army":

> All the real heroes are not storybook combat fighters.
> Every single man in the army plays a vital role. So don't
> ever let up. Don't ever think that your job is unimportant.

What if every truck driver decided that he didn't like the whine of the shells and turned yellow and jumped headlong into a ditch? That cowardly bastard could say to himself, "Hell, they won't miss me, just one man in thousands." What if every man said that? Where in the hell would we be then? No, thank God, Americans don't say that. Every man does his job. Every man is important. The ordnance men are needed to supply the guns, the quartermaster is needed to bring up the food and clothes for us because where we are going there isn't a hell of a lot to steal. Every last damn man in the mess hall, even the one who boils the water to keep us from getting the GI shits, has a job to do.

....

CHAPTER FOUR

The Unforgiving Minute

If Patton's faults were clearly demonstrated by his disrespect toward his superiors, there was no doubting his battlefield acumen. Patton's genius lay in his ability to identify the right moment to thrust against the enemy. He knew the value of what his favorite poet, Rudyard Kipling, called the "unforgiving minute." Once Patton decided to attack, he did not stop. His philosophy of war was purely focused on the offensive—hardly surprising, given his training as a cavalryman and his reputation as a tanker.

As historian Victor Davis Hanson notes, Patton appreciated the Kipling maxim, knowing that "in war, you get one chance and one chance only, and it's a split second. Fortune favors the brave, the audacious people. If you're a clerk, you can come up with a thousand reasons that are quite logical and quite legalistic and bureaucratic not to take a risk." This same maxim Patton could have pulled off his own bookshelf, from the works of Frederick the Great, who affirmed, "The Prussian army always attacks."

Patton disdained passive defense and saw caution and balance as flaws in commanders. Indeed, he regularly criticized his superiors for not pressing their advantage. For example, he saw both Eisenhower and Bradley as indecisive. Sometimes, his overcautious superiors either commanded or forced him to halt before reaching his objective. This occurred several times throughout the war, with one especially poignant instance taking place shortly after he resumed operations on the Continent.

Back in the Saddle

One month after the invasion of Normandy, there was little progress from the beachheads. Bradley was stuck in the massive hedgerows of boscage country, and Montgomery was pinned down at Caen. Finally, in early July, Patton was unleashed from his decoy role in the Allies' campaign, and the Third Army was ordered to join Omar Bradley's First Army in Normandy. Bradley had been

> apprehensive in having George join my command, for I feared that too much of my time would probably be spent curbing his impetuous habits. But at the same time I knew that with Patton there would be no need for my whipping Third Army to keep it on the move. We had only to keep him pointed in the direction we wanted to go.

Bradley soon recognized that he was wrong to hold such "uncharitable reservations, for he [Patton] not only bore me no ill will but he trooped for 12th Army Group with unbounded loyalty and eagerness." In a matter of months, "the new Patton had totally obliterated my [Bradley's] unwarranted apprehensions; we formed as amiable and contented a team as existed in the senior command. . . . George had now become a serious, reasonable, and likable commander."

Patton was thrilled to be back in action. He told his men, "I'm proud to be here to fight beside you. Now let's cut the guts out of those Krauts and get the hell to Berlin. And when we get to Berlin, I am going to personally shoot that paper-hanging goddamned son of a bitch"—that is, Hitler. In his diary, Patton would write:

[W]e had a new preacher, at my insistence, who was good.
He preached on the willingness to accept responsibility,
even to your own hurt. That ability is what we need and
what Ike lacks. But I do feel that I don't. I pray daily to
do my duty, retain my self-confidence, and accomplish
my destiny. No one can live under the awful responsibility
that I have without Divine help. Frequently I feel that I
don't rate it.

The problem confronting the Allies at this juncture was the difficult terrain of northern France. First, the marshy ground impeded
movement. Second, and far more important, there were the massive, thick hedgerows. These obstacles were doubly problematic, as
they gave the Germans cover—allowing them to harass the advancing Anglo-American forces in a slow, fighting retreat—and they
were impermeable to tanks. Whenever a tank would attempt to
drive through one of the hedgerows, its nose was forced into the
air, exposing its unarmored bottom to enemy fires. This challenge
seemed insurmountable until Bradley became aware of a sergeant's
innovative approach to enabling tanks to break through the hedgerows by attaching prongs, comparable to those seen on a forklift, to
the front of those vehicles. This kept the tanks from going nose-up.
Bradley ordered the mass production of these prongs, which were
also referred to as "tusks" and "hedgerow cutters."

The use of these prongs on the tanks, which came to be known
as "rhinos," allowed Bradley to plan a breakthrough in the German
line, which he hoped would give the Allied forces some breathing
room. His plan, code-named Operation Cobra, would use strategic bombers and fighter-bombers to pound a hole in the German
line, through which the massed forces of J. Lawton "Lightning Joe"
Collins's VII Corps would rush, in hopes of reaching more favo-
rable territory for maneuver. This was an unconventional design,

as the payloads of strategic bombers were so large as to present the dual risks of hitting friendly units and slowing their movements by creating craters and debris, thereby allowing the enemy to regroup and settle into new defensive positions. Bradley accepted these risks.

Operation Cobra was scheduled to begin on July 24, but poor weather conditions forced Bradley to postpone it until the next day. As fate would have it, the halt order did not reach the bombers in England in time, and they ruined the element of surprise by beginning their bombing without ground forces being prepared to advance through the gaps. Furthermore, some friendly troops were actually hit by the bombings. The next day, however, Operation Cobra began. Though the first day of the operation appeared to be yet another failed breakthrough in the face of sustained German defenses, the reality was far different: The German line was about to break. Having made some progress, Collins gambled, ordering his armored units through the gap without adequate support for an exploitation. This proved to be the deciding factor in Operation Cobra. Bradley, realizing that he needed to exploit the break-through, decided on July 28 that Patton was just the man for the job and told him to prepare the Third Army for action.

Energized by a return to action, Patton knew exactly what he needed to do: "Rush them off their feet before they get set." In an address to his officers the night before they began operations, he flippantly dismissed caution, telling them, "Forget this goddamn business of worrying about our flanks, but not to the extent we don't do anything else." Patton then graphically described what his Third Army was to do to the enemy: "We're going to kick the hell out of him all the time and we're going to go through him like crap through a goose." This hard-driving attitude would serve him well, making August 1944 what Carlo D'Este considers "the turning point in Patton's fortunes and . . . the most electrifying and rewarding month of his career."

At noon on August 1, Patton's Third Army began operations. Under his command, the Third Army exploited gaps in the German line and then swept across the French countryside, chasing the German Army. In a run characterized by speed and coordination and employing the advance-attack-advance-and-attack-again formula, Patton helped consummate the transformation of Bradley's somewhat modest breakthrough plan with Operation Cobra into a spectacular breakout.

Third Army advanced so rapidly in early August that its command post had to be relocated every night. As Patton's commanding officer, General Omar Bradley, later put it, Patton "push[ed] 200,000 men and 40,000 vehicles through what amounted to a straw" on the single road to the French town of Avranches. When his bold, swift maneuver resulted in serious traffic jams in Avranches, Patton himself directed traffic, thereby saving the efficiency in the Third Army's lightning advance. His speedy offensive resulted in other logistical problems, however, as the Fourth and Sixth Armored Divisions outran their lines of communication, making coordination difficult.

Riding High

Though for a time the Third Army ran amok over the peninsulas of Brittany and Cotentin in western France, Patton's superiors, specifically Bradley, soon pulled on the reins, concerned that Patton might overextend himself. Patton was irritated but did not speak out openly against his commanders, fearful of being removed once more. Writing of his desire to press on toward Nantes, Patton confided to his diary, "I am sure he [Bradley] would think it too risky. It is slightly risky, but so is war." Just the day before, he had complained about the caution of his superiors, disclosing how he was "disgusted with human frailty. However, the lambent flame of my own self-confidence burns ever brighter." Clearly, Patton's ego grew unabated, as he relished being back in action, to the point that he seemingly did not care if he was fighting in the right direction. As historian Russell F. Weigley argues, Patton's tactic of "charging in all directions at the same time" effectively "distract[ed] the Allies from their main offensive purpose, which should have been to pursue the German armies toward their destruction." Weigley notes, however, that "Patton's aggressiveness, also helped stimulate movement in the proper direction of opportunity and ultimate purpose" when he turned the Cobra breakthrough into a breakout.

So Patton reined in his subordinates and forced them to follow Bradley's orders to clear the rest of the Germans out of Brittany before turning eastward. Bradley's decision to focus attention on northwest France prior to moving eastward toward Paris and (eventually) the German border became one of the most highly criticized strategic decisions of the war, as it demonstrated his inflexibility, since he refused to deviate from the Overlord plans, despite the circumstances. Gen. John Shirley "Tiger Jack" Wood, commander of the Fourth Armored Division under Patton, was furious with Patton's orders to continue sweeping through northwest France, complaining to Gen. Troy Middleton, "We're winning this war the wrong way, we ought to be going toward Paris." Wood also let Patton know that he was enraged, sending him a sarcastic message that read, "Trust we can turn around and get headed in the right direction soon." Patton later informed Wood, "You almost got tried for that [message]." Wood replied, "Someone should have been tried but it certainly was not I." Little did Wood know, however, that Patton also felt Bradley's strategy was a foolhardy one but could not say so due to his precarious position in the command structure.

Bradley wanted to slow down for fear of outrunning supply lines, which he considered "the lifeblood of the Allied armies in

France." But in time, he realized that he needed to turn the Allied forces toward the east, much to Patton's delight. Patton saw the Wehrmacht crumbling before the Allied advance and even confided to Beatrice that the German enemy "is finished. We may end this in ten days." So rapid was the move east that within a week of writing that letter to his wife, Patton wrote in his diary, "In exactly two weeks the Third Army has advanced farther and faster than any Army in the history of war." His Day with Destiny was back on track.

Much of the credit for this achievement went to Patton, who scorned traditional notions of securing flanks, instead preferring to advance whenever and wherever possible, flanks be damned. Indeed, Patton was so unconcerned with his flanks that he always led from the front, spearheading the advance of his Third Army. His thinking on the subject is well summarized in a quote he regularly gave to both the press—with whom he was now wildly popular—and his men: "If you want an army to fight and risk death, you've got to get up there and lead it. An army is like spaghetti. You can't push a piece of spaghetti, you've got to pull it."

Patton's penchant for seemingly ignoring his flanks was hardly a reckless or rash decision, however. He was able to employ such an aggressive strategy for two key reasons: intelligence and close air support. Over the course of the Normandy campaign, Patton developed a close friendship with Gen. Otto P. "Opie" Weyland, commander of the XIX Tactical Air Command, or TAC, Army Air Corps. The tremendous coordination of air and ground forces resulting from their blossoming friendship made it possible for Patton to receive both aerial reconnaissance reports to help him plan maneuvers and close air support to soften up the enemy before the Third Army arrived. Once, when asked whether he worried about his flanks, Patton replied in the negative, saying, "The Air

Force takes care of my flanks." Additionally, Patton had other intelligence sources, such as French Resistance fighters and Ultra intercepts of German military communications. He was careful to take all of these factors into consideration before making his next move. As such, while Patton was certainly the most aggressive American general in the war, he did not simply rely upon blind thrusts to speed the Third Army along. Rather, like any good general, he considered intelligence reports and coordinated his actions with those of the Army Air Corps. Indeed, in this latter regard he was ahead of his time, as the American military would struggle to coordinate air and ground forces in a number of conflicts after World War II, with the most infamous examples in Vietnam (1964–1975) and especially Grenada (1983).

The notion of Patton being on the road to redemption was confirmed by his promotion to four-star general, though Eisenhower warned him, "General Marshall has asked that you not spoil the record of a magnificent job by public statements," reminding Patton that he was still on a short leash. Shortly after learning of his promotion, which would officially go into effect on September 2, he was informed that he would not be the one to liberate Paris; that honor would fall to Gen. Jacques Leclerc of the Free French 2nd Armored Division. Patton was extremely disappointed, and his staff, in Robert S. Allen's words, "regarded the decision as the last straw in Eisenhower's increasingly apparent measures to exclude Patton from the glory road."

In an effort to maintain the secrecy of Allied planning, the press corps had been forbidden from reporting on Patton's moves until, on August 15, it was publicly announced that Patton was the commander of the Third Army, of which the Germans were already painfully aware.

A Missed Opportunity

As Patton and the Allies began moving east, they quickly discovered that they were surrounding the Wehrmacht in France and that they had a chance to encircle and crush their enemy in a manner reminiscent of Hannibal's legendary double envelopment at Cannae. Bradley, thrilled at the chance to make military history, described the situation as "an opportunity that comes to a commander not more than once in a century." To complete the encirclement, the Allies needed to close what came to be known as the "Falaise Pocket," so named because the "bottom" of the pocket was supposed to be between the French towns of Falaise and Argentan. (It is sometimes called the Falaise-Argentan Pocket.)

While the Allies began closing in, Hitler made one of the most criticized military decisions of the war. He ignored the advice of his top military advisers—most of whom advocated for a withdrawal of German forces from Normandy and even France, so as to consolidate in a better defensive position—and decided not only to keep the Wehrmacht in France but also to launch a counterattack at Mortain, code-named Operation Lüttich. As Martin Blumenson writes, "The solution [Hitler] imposed was unorthodox, but hardly mad. His concept contained a well-reasoned logic." For one thing, throughout the course of the war, the Fuhrer had increasingly made the military decisions, seeing his general staff more as executors than as advisers or policymakers. To compound the situation, an officer-led assassination attempt on July 20 had made him substantially more wary of his military advisers. Additionally, he had accepted that the Balkans and Finland would soon slip from the German grip, while the situations on the Eastern and Italian fronts were seemingly under control. As such, his "most pressing concern was France." Meanwhile, withdrawal was less profitable than his general staff seemed to think, as there were no readily defensible areas in the rear areas. Thus, to Hitler, a counterattack made the most sense.

In fact, the counterattack proved devastating. Hitler did not know that the Allies would intercept the orders for the maneuver using their Ultra program. Once Bradley and Patton learned of the Lüttich plan, they knew they had to act quickly to capitalize on Hitler's blunder; indeed, Bradley called it the "[g]reatest tactical blunder I've ever heard of," predicting that something like it "probably won't happen again in a thousand years." The German counterattack on August 8 failed miserably, as coordination of air and ground forces quickly blunted the thrust, though Hitler insisted on continuing the attack, demanding a breakthrough at Mortain. That worsened the German situation, however, as it effectively "pushed the leading German combat units into a noose that the Allies would try to close."

On the same morning as Operation Lüttich, Montgomery launched Operation Totalize, which sent the II Canadian Corps under Lt. Gen. Guy Simonds from Caen down to Falaise. If successful, Totalize would complete the Allies' encirclement of the Germans, setting the stage for their destruction. Assuming the Canadians would reach Falaise, Eisenhower, Montgomery, and Bradley ordered Patton to redirect Gen. Wade Haislip's XV Corps from its initial eastward push toward Le Mans to the north, using Le Mans as the pivot point, with Argentan as its new objective. This would complete the double envelopment, with the II Canadian Corps and the American XV Corps serving as short hooks. Patton, however, insisted on a deeper envelopment, in which Haislip's XV Corps and Gen. Walton Walker's XX Corps, acting as a long hook, would push further east to Chartres or Dreux and then turn north to complete the encirclement. Bradley disagreed, and Patton complied, ordering Haislip toward Argentan.

By August 13, XV Corps was nearly to Argentan, as it maintained its inertia in what Patton called "probably the fastest and biggest pursuit in history." Unfortunately, XV Corps' advance was halted before reaching Argentan because it had already passed the unofficial army group boundary established by Montgomery in an effort to keep the American and British (including Canadian) armies from running into one another. Since the Canadians still had not reached Falaise due to a series of accidents, Patton argued that Haislip could quickly push north toward Falaise, sealing both the Pocket and the German forces' fate. Unfortunately, Bradley ordered Patton to stand down, as his intelligence led him to believe the Germans might attempt to break through between Patton's Third Army in the east and Gen. Courtney Hodges' First Army to the west. He wanted to respect Montgomery's line, thinking that the British field marshal would invite the American troops across it. Due to bad intelligence, Bradley also thought the Germans were hurriedly escaping through the Falaise-Argentan gap, when, in reality, they were pushing against the inside of the pocket, hoping to keep it from collapsing before Hitler gave the withdrawal order. Of the decision, Patton wrote, "This corps could easily advance to Falaise and completely close the gap, but we have been ordered to halt because the British sowed the area between with a large number of time bombs. I am sure that this halt is a great mistake, as I am certain that the [Canadians] will not close on Falaise."

Patton, hoping to salvage the situation, convinced Bradley to let him send a few corps east to Dreux, Chartres, and Orléans, breathing new life into Patton's previously discarded "long hook" concept. Patton wrote of his conversation with Bradley, "It really is a great plan, wholly my own, and I made Bradley think he thought of it. 'Oh, what a tangled web we weave when first we practice to deceive.' I am very happy and elated." He ordered XV Corps, XX

Corps, and XII Corps east on August 14; they reached their objectives by August 16.

Bradley was still cautious, however, ordering Patton to halt his advance due to intelligence reports about a unit of Panzers at Argentan, leading Patton to opine that Bradley's "motto seems to be, 'In case of doubt, halt'" and complain that "I [Patton] wish I were Supreme Commander." After arriving at Argentan, Patton established a provisional headquarters and ordered an attack for the morning of August 17. The attack was canceled, however, when Gen. Leonard Gerow, of the First Army's V Corps, arrived to assume command of the Argentan front. Gerow disapproved of the plan that Patton's chief of staff, Gen. Hugh Gaffey, had formulated, so he scrapped it and planned his own attack for August 18. Gerow's decision to delay closing the short hooks exacerbated the failure of the double envelopment, as over 100,000 German soldiers escaped through the gap, despite losing 50,000 of their comrades in the process. Thus ended the abortive double envelopment of the Falaise Pocket.

The decision to halt Patton's advance at several points during the attempt to close the Falaise Pocket would haunt Eisenhower, as many of these 250,000 German soldiers later regrouped to challenge the Allies at the Battle of the Bulge just six months later, where Hitler, with unfettered Panzer fury, 88-mm guns, and Screaming Mimi rockets, made one last thrust against the Allies. American soldiers, who had been assured by Eisenhower that Ardennes was a place for rest and knew Bradley's belief that "the roads are much too scarce, the hills too wooded, and the valleys too limited for maneuver," would pay a bloody price.

Restraint

It was not the last time that Patton's destiny would be impeded. In late August, as he approached the strongholds of Nancy and

Metz, Patton was informed that Eisenhower had cut off his gasoline and supplies, favoring the needs of Field Marshal Montgomery and Operation Market Garden, even as Patton was within striking distance of the Siegfried Line. At a meeting with Eisenhower and Bradley on August 19, Monty proposed an offensive involving a single thrust toward Antwerp and the Ruhr River by the Canadian First Army, the British Second Army, and the U.S. First Army; the Fourth Allied Army on the Continent, which just happened to be Patton's Third, would stay back to hold a position on the Meuse River. While Montgomery compared his proposal to the famous German Schlieffen Plan that predated World War I, it reminded Bradley "of Monty's tactics during the Sicilian campaign when he recommended that U.S. forces sit out the war on a defensive front while he went on alone to take Messina." Montgomery clearly wanted to exclude Patton.

The American plan, put forward by Bradley and Eisenhower, entailed a broad-front, double-thrust approach. Rather than giving Montgomery all of the U.S. First Army for his advance toward the Ruhr, he would receive one corps from that formation. The Canadian and British forces would still advance in a manner similar to that proposed by Monty, but the remainder of U.S. First Army and U.S. Third Army would thrust toward Mainz and the Saar River, toward (and through) the southern portion of the Siegfried Line.

Quarreling over the competing plans for the Siegfried Line campaign was bitter. While Montgomery involved Prime Minister Churchill in the operational debate, Patton proposed that he, Bradley, and Gen. Courtney Hodges threaten to resign if Ike chose Montgomery's plan, assuming that "in such a showdown we would win, as Ike would not dare to relieve us." Bradley, however, declined, saying they "owed it to the troops to hold on, because if we left, the pickings [other jobs] were poor." Patton thought this argument was disingenuous but decided to drop the matter. The chief of the Imperial General Staff, Field Marshal Alan Brooke, thought the American plan would extend the war by "three to six months." On August 23, the same day Patton pitched his resignation threat plan to Bradley, Eisenhower tentatively decided in favor of Montgomery's plan.

Patton knew that Eisenhower had caved into Churchill, allowing Montgomery to lead the charge across the Rhine, thinking that "public opinion wins wars." If the Germans could not stop Patton, Allied logistics could—and did. On the Meuse, at the end of August, the Third Army outran its gasoline. Germany lay just beyond reach, with its vaunted Siegfried Line, the country's main western defensive wall, virtually unmanned. Given 400,000 gallons of gasoline, Patton told Bradley, he could be in Germany within two days. Unfortunately, he did not receive that fuel.

By the end of September, the flow of supplies declined again, and Patton was forced to accept what his superiors called the "October pause." As much as Patton loathed being forced to slow his advance, this was essentially a logistical problem; the Allied forces were constrained by their dependence on the ports at Arromanches and Cherbourg on the Cotentin Peninsula in western France. Although the Allies captured Antwerp and its port on September 4, they could not use the port to resupply without first clearing the Scheldt Estuary of German troops.

The Scheldt operation was delayed because Montgomery chose to focus his efforts on the ill-fated Operation Market Garden in September. While he took responsibility, Montgomery blamed the operation's failure largely on insufficient supplies, men, and aircraft, in addition to poor weather and mistaken Allied assessments of German strength, especially in Arnhem. To his dying day, Montgomery "remain[ed] Market Garden's unrepentant advocate."

Eisenhower, as the commander of Allied forces in Western Europe, also took the blame for the operation's failure, saying, "If I had not attempted the Arnhem operation," the Allies could have maintained their momentum more effectively. Spurred by Bradley's admonition to get most of the Third Army across the Moselle River, Patton covered an amazing 50 miles in two days. Unfortunately, his supplies had been wearing thin, and he was forced to halt. "Patton," Bradley later recalled, "had finally reached the end of his tether."

Patton wrote to Beatrice: "Going on the defense and having our limited supplies cut still more is very discouraging. Bradley and I are depressed. We would like to go to China and serve under Admiral [Chester] Nimitz." Indeed, adopting a defensive posture went against every fiber of Patton's being; he was an attacker, born for the offensive. Passive defense disgusted him. He kept his head up, however, and presented a lighthearted disposition at a press conference two days later, saying, "I always feel at these meetings we should have on black hoods over our heads as in the Inquisition." When asked how he intended to proceed, Patton, true to form, said: "It is my earnest effort to keep it from becoming static because that is a poor way of fighting. The best way to defend is to attack, and the best way to attack is to attack."

A desperate Patton was forced to use his own money as a bribe for gasoline to allow his armored vehicles to continue forward. Despite the lack of gasoline, Patton beat Monty across the Rhine, just as he had beaten him in the race to Messina.

Eisenhower preferred a broad-front advance, even if it meant slowing down Patton's progress so that other Allied forces could catch up. What resulted was a logistical nightmare as critical supplies lagged behind combat forces. A frustrated Patton remarked: "Ike is all for caution since he has never been at the front and has no feel of actual fighting. Bradley, Hodges, and I are all for a prompt advance." Patton was a lifelong student of battle and understood the importance of being prepared and ready for action at all times.

Historian Victor Davis Hanson reminds us: "For all his excesses, Patton empathized with his soldiers. And he was scientific and logical about his empathy. He wanted them to change their socks. He wanted them to keep clean, know how to use their rifle. He wanted to make sure they didn't get frost bite." The other commanders never even thought about the practical matters. But Patton did, and it endeared him to his men.

In fact, the "men" under Patton's command were barely more than boys. He understood what made them tick and how to motivate them. "Patton had a very unique idea that when you're moving and you're active, 18-year-olds don't get in trouble," notes Hanson. Patton knew instinctively that when the young men of war are "sitting around entrenched, then by nature they're mischievous and are not used to their maximum potential. He was thinking, got to move, got to move, got to move."

Patton's admonishments to his men, at times, resembled that of pure fatherly confidence or a pep talk heard during a football game. "An army is a team," he would say.

> It lives, eats, sleeps, and fights as a team. This individual hero stuff is bullshit. The bilious bastards who write that stuff for the *Saturday Evening Post* don't know any more about real battle than they do about fucking. And we have the best team—we have the finest food and equipment, the best spirit and the best men in the world. Why, by God, I actually pity these poor bastards we're going up against.

It was a well-prepared Patton who rescued Eisenhower and the Allies in the bitter cold winter of 1944–1945 in what became known as the Battle of the Bulge. On December 16, Hitler launched

Operation Autumn Mist, an all-out offensive against Gen. Troy H. Middleton's VIII Corps. The First U.S. Army, covering the Ardennes Forest in Luxembourg, neared the town of Bastogne. Before Eisenhower even knew to request it, Patton had planned a response. Bradley asked Patton what he could send and when. Without hesitation, Patton replied that he could send three divisions immediately—one starting off at midnight, the next at first light, and the third within 24 hours. It was a remarkable promise to make and one he would fulfill.

In this moment, one can imagine Patton consulting with the great military giants. As Martin Blumenson writes, "In the winter time, Caesar so trained his legions in all that became soldiers and so habituated them in the proper performance of their duties, that when in the spring he committed them to battle against the Gauls, it was not necessary to give them orders, for they knew what to do and how to do it."

In blizzard-like conditions, Patton led his men northward in a valiant effort to halt the German offensive. He later bragged, "I think that this move of the Third Army is the fastest in history. We moved over a hundred miles starting on the 19th and attacked to day [sic] all ship shape and Bristol fashion." Patton and his men saved the Allies from what would certainly have been a crushing defeat that would have split the U.S. and British armies and tipped the war on the Western Front back in Hitler's favor.

Yet months later, after Patton's heroic and critical detour north through the Ardennes, the Third Army's push toward the Rhine was stunted once again due to the logistical failures of High Command. Once the threat to Bastogne had been vanquished, the other commanders, especially Eisenhower and Bradley, lost the momentum that had been created by the crisis. A frustrated Patton wrote: "The 6th Army Group is to go on the defensive. . . . Personally, I think that this is a foolish and ignoble way for the Americans to end the war. In my opinion, every division should be attacking, and if such an attack were made, the Germans do not have the resources to stop it." Albert Speer, the architect of the Third Reich, had already told Hitler, on January 30, 1945, that the war was unwinnable, and for the weary German people, surrender to the Allies was preferable to defeat at the hands of the Red Army fighting its way to Berlin to avenge the Soviet Union's losses.

Patton was beside himself.

CHAPTER FIVE

....

The Puppeteers

On and off the battlefield, Patton was a force to be reckoned with. Yet the very qualities that made Patton a successful battlefield general—unflinching nerve, audacity, and fearless candor—were the same characteristics that made him a nuisance when the fighting was over. This paradox, of course, is the tragic certainty of any antihero.

On the ground, Patton was a formidable asset for the Allies, a hard-charging war machine feared and admired by his men and his opponents. In the war rooms and central command, however, these same qualities made Patton a liability. He lacked diplomacy, and his actions bordered on insubordination. His reputation for clashing with authority climbed the chain of command from Ike to Marshall and others, including Roosevelt.

For all his bravado and sense of destiny, in the greater context Patton would be constrained time and again by the military apparatus to which he was devoted. As leading military historian Dennis Showalter surmised, Patton was "merely a saxophonist" in the big band that was the Allied command structure. Throughout the war, his sense of destiny would be thwarted and defined by the orchestrations of the decision makers—the puppeteers.

The Big Three

Orson Welles, the great film director and campaigner, said, "Roosevelt used to say to me, 'You and I are the two best actors in America.'" Indeed, one of Roosevelt's greatest legacies proved to be his ability to communicate with people, whether high government officials or common constituents. His fabled fireside chats and comforting rhetoric during the darkest days of war united a nation and inspired a generation. While he rhetorically supported the Constitution and confronted the despotic Nazi regime, he seemed slow to the microphone when it came to communism.

Roosevelt believed he had a special rapport with Stalin, despite the obvious disparity in core ideologies between the two. Roosevelt was under the dangerous illusion that he knew how to handle Stalin, when, in fact, it was Stalin who knew how to play Roosevelt. In the dynamics of the Big Three, it is Roosevelt who emerges as, what some would describe, a Soviet sympathizer. Roosevelt, along with trusted advisers such as Harry Hopkins and Henry Dexter White, was downright charmed by Stalin, whom he affectionately called "Uncle Joe." Roosevelt was of the firm belief that, in time, he could transform the tyrant into a "Christian gentlemen." Toward that end and before critical discussions at Yalta about postwar world order commenced, Roosevelt wedged Churchill out of the conversation so that he might meet with Stalin alone. The result: though Roosevelt persistently voiced great distaste for the British Empire, his unabashed attraction to Stalin enabled the rise of a new and dangerous Soviet empire.

The myth that FDR had the upper hand in his dealings with Stalin has been well preserved. After more than seven decades, conventional wisdom continues to turn a blind eye toward the true nature of the relationship between the two leaders. Instead, focus persists on such trivialities as Churchill's "naughty document," credited by many as providing the mechanism for carving up postwar geopolitical boundaries. To many, Roosevelt's alleged enchantment with the dictator remains a clever ruse, a public display of master stagecraft. But 75 years of history hence, we can recognize that FDR's fond words for Josef Stalin go well beyond politics or war. As historian Paul Kengor writes in *Dupes: How America's Adversaries Have Manipulated Progressives for a Century*:

> The President very often used words of eye opening personal affection. Only three months after Pearl Harbor, for example, FDR wrote a note to Winston Churchill in anticipation of his first meeting with Stalin. "I think I can personally handle Stalin better than your Foreign Office or my State Department," FDR boasted to Churchill on March 18, 1942. "Stalin hates the guts of all your people. He thinks he likes me better."

Some observers aim to protect the FDR myth—that Roosevelt genuinely believed in his ability to shape and influence Stalin's thinking—by suggesting that failing health and exhaustion from the war may have clouded his judgment, causing him to develop a myopic view of the Russian tyrant. Few would argue that fatigue would not have contributed to the state of Roosevelt's mind, though Churchill also suffered from fatigue, but without the same lack of judgment. Yet Roosevelt also rejected the warnings from some of his closest advisers. As early as 1941, Roosevelt's former Soviet Ambassador William Bullitt, Jr., who had his own "Bolshevik romance" but later came to his senses, tried to warn Roosevelt that "Communists in the United States are just as dangerous enemies as ever" and that his policies were "wishful thinking."

In return for his candor, Bullitt received this wishful reply from the president: "I just have a hunch that Stalin is not that kind of man. . . . I think that if I give him everything I possibly can and ask nothing in return, noblesse oblige, he won't try to annex anything and will work with me for a world of democracy and peace."

Unlike the president, Churchill held his nose and dealt with Stalin only when necessary and with grave reservation. He did not relish his dealings with "the devil," nor did he welcome any personal challenge to find "Uncle Joe's" good graces. He was under no illusions that he (or anyone else) could change Stalin's nature. Churchill, to his credit, wanted the Allies to capture Berlin, to defend Prague and the rest of Eastern Europe, and he urged Allied forces to "meet the Red Army as far east as possible," which meant capturing the key capitals. Churchill understood that the wholesale offering of Berlin—the crown jewel of Europe—would give Stalin the upper hand in postwar power. By contrast, Roosevelt defended Stalin's honor and called for Eisenhower to avoid any contact with Russians, handing over Berlin as merely a symbolic gesture. Thus did Eisenhower and his generals look away at what would become the rape and slaughter of more than 11 million people at the hands of the "liberating" Soviets.

Relinquishing Berlin to the Russians was not only a grave error, demonstrating Roosevelt's alarming lack of knowledge of history and geography and lack of common sense, it was, as British historian Antony Beevor notes, "unthinkable that the Western Allies simply could not hope to push back the Red Army" to their original borders. Failing to do so emboldened the Russians to not only snatch Berlin as a strategic target but also positioned them to topple other Eastern European governments. Likewise, as a result of Roosevelt's policies that were passed down the line of command through Marshall and Eisenhower on the battlefield, the Soviets found, outside Berlin, the resources needed to begin amassing the nuclear arsenal that would figure prominently in the coming Cold War with the United States.

Still, despite warnings from William Bullitt, Winston Churchill, and even Gen. George S. Patton, Roosevelt maintained there was nothing he could not do with the misguided Russian tyrant. While the myth prior to the end of World War II might have held truths that reflected the facts about Roosevelt's presidency and his efforts to hold a country together through difficult times, many would argue that there is no excuse for his naïveté (or perhaps hubris) in dealing with Stalin, which resulted in the devastating betrayal of the people of Berlin, Eastern Europe, and even the United States. Roosevelt's uplifting rhetoric helped American's endure a treacherous moment in our collective history as we sacrificed the lives of hundreds of thousands of American soldiers for what most believed to be the true cause of freedom. Yet Roosevelt's myth of Stalin as a trustworthy partner in postwar Europe was born of illusion, or a delusion, later proven wrong by the facts. Stalin broke every agreement he had made, he slaughtered tens of millions of people in his scourge of German, Polish, and Ukrainian citizenry in the newly occupied lands, not to mention the utter horrors that occurred back in his own gulags, where millions more were taken prisoner, including 20,000 Allied POWs.

We do not need a slanted storyteller to make the case for Roosevelt's self-deception. Roosevelt himself recognized his mistake—albeit too late—as noted by former U.S. Ambassador to the Soviet Union Averell Harriman: "On March 23, 1945, Roosevelt confided to Anna Rosenberg, a well-known businesswoman and public official during the war, 'Averell is right. We can't do business with Stalin. He has broken every one of the promises he made at Yalta.'" But where was the surprise? How else could Roosevelt have imagined the outcome, trusting a man who had already killed tens of millions of his own people to establish his coming empire? What good were Roosevelt's words when his basic judgment would allow a monster like Stalin to feed on the millions of innocents in Eastern Europe and enable the Cold War?

As historian Kengor concludes, "[FDR's] appraisal of Stalin was one of the most naïve assessments of any major foreign leader in the history of the American presidency." When the facts so undermine this narrative or myth, it is rightfully time for that myth to be set aside for a more precise explanation, as will be the case with Roosevelt. Myths are not lies. And they are not created to deceive but rather to communicate a higher truth. This does not mean they are factually accurate or meant to last forever, a point missed by many ideologues even in academia. And while academia tries to limit itself to the empirical evidence or to know how to interpret facts, these facts require a context or, in the case of a story, a real-world narrative. As we revisit the triumphs and blunders of the twentieth century, Roosevelt's naïve relationship with Stalin and the horrific Cold War legacy that resulted are evidence of a very costly enchantment.

Many historians, such as Paul Kengor, believe the FDR administration was conspicuously soft on communism. According to Kengor, there were many Soviet sympathizers and even outright spies within the administration's ranks. "All of these people would have been outright hostile to someone like George Patton," he says. "They would have seen him as an absolute menace."

Roosevelt prioritized winning the war above all other foreign policy considerations. This did not mean, however, that he ignored the problem of postwar Soviet power. Although he shied away from the use of military force to contain the Soviets in the Balkans and Eastern Europe, the president, less than a week before his death in April 1945, assured Churchill that "our armies will in a very few days be in a position that will permit us to become 'tougher' [on the Soviets] than has heretofore appeared advantageous to the war effort."

While "Roosevelt did not orient wartime strategy toward the coming Cold War," rejecting containment via military or exhaustion (i.e., letting the Red Army weaken itself through fighting), he seemingly planned to limit Soviet power through "containment by integration." This strategy depended on Roosevelt's assumption that the Soviets were hostile because they felt threatened by external forces; as such, the president worked to incorporate them into the postwar system through his "Four Policemen" framework. This vision of the postwar order placed the United States, Great Britain, China, and the Soviet Union as the four strongest states in the system, enshrined in their permanent status on the UN Security Council. By incorporating the USSR into this postwar order, Roosevelt hoped to curb Stalin's appetites. Unfortunately, he was mistaken.

Churchill, on the other hand, had grave reservations about Stalin and was reluctant to work with the brutal dictator, viewing their alliance as one of necessity that was not to be continued after the war. This created friction between the English and American leaders, which was worsened by Roosevelt's strong desire to dismantle European empires, including that of the British. FDR's vision for a world without empires—a continuation of Woodrow Wilson's notion of "making the world safe for democracy"—was formally expressed in the Atlantic Charter, signed by both himself and Churchill in August 1941, months before the United States entered the war. This Anglo-American agreement promised, among other things, that the two great powers would "respect the right of all peoples to choose the form of government under which they will live; and they wish to see sovereign rights and self-government restored to those who have been forcibly deprived of them." This clause effectively indicated that empires would not be tolerated in the postwar world, a fact of which Churchill was painfully aware. As such, he sought to protect British imperial interest throughout the war, although his efforts ultimately met with mixed success.

With the German Wehrmacht at the gates of Stalingrad, the namesake of that city continued to press for increased Allied aid to the Soviet Union, in the form of supplies, materiel, and—most important—the opening of a second front against the German menace. Although Anglo-American forces had begun moving toward Italy with the invasion of North Africa in late 1942, Stalin demanded that more be done, not least because of the numerous delays in the opening of an effective second front, which had been promised since earlier that year.

Thus began a series of diplomatic summits between the Big Three, designed to better coordinate their strategies. The first conference, held in Casablanca in the winter of 1943, was attended by Roosevelt and Churchill only. Stalin would join his cohorts in the following two summits, in Tehran in late 1943 and Yalta in February 1945. The policies born of these meetings would shape the geopolitical postwar order. For Patton, many of the strategic decisions agreed to were untenable and contrary to his vision of a proper postwar resolution. This disparity would put him frequently at odds with his superiors and would create a tension between his own sense of destiny and the orders he was charged with implementing.

Casablanca 1943

Roosevelt and Churchill met at Casablanca on January 14 to set the course for Allied military strategy in Europe and Asia. Though Stalin could not attend due to the pending fight in Stalingrad, his influence was felt at the conference. The meeting, code-named SYMBOL, primarily consisted of Anglo-American military planning. Patton helped Gen. Mark Clark host the British and American heads of state but wrote to Beatrice that he was very grateful to not be involved in the "great and very hush hush conference." Instead, he was charged with providing security for the various British and American officials meeting there and entertaining them. Patton was quite nervous that the secret conference would be attacked by Axis bombers, so he ordered the construction of an air raid shelter for Roosevelt and Churchill using concrete, sandbags, and steel. Despite his anxieties over the safety of the conferees, Patton was flabbergasted by Clark's proposal that American soldiers be stationed at El Hank, south of Casablanca, to ensure that the French guns there were not turned on the site of the Allied meetings. He "argued him out of the idea," threatening to resign if such action were taken, as "[i]t would have been the crowning insult to the French and would have given the Nazis a wonderful propaganda weapon and roused the Arabs."

While Patton was correct in deducing that the French would have been insulted by Clark's proposed measures to control the French gunners, Clark had reason for concern. On July 3, 1940, more than 1,000 French sailors had been killed when a British naval unit destroyed a Vichy French naval squadron at Mers-el-Kébir in an attack that came to be known as the "French Pearl Harbor." Churchill had ordered the attack, hoping to keep the French vessels out of German hands and to signal to FDR that he had the resolve to oppose the German menace at all costs. As such, it would have been reasonable for Clark to be concerned that had the French gunners at El Hank learned of Churchill's presence at the Casablanca Conference, they may have opened fire on the city in a bid to avenge their fallen comrades.

During the course of the conference, Patton rubbed elbows with a number of important figures from the British and American governments and militaries. When he met Sir Dudley Pound and Sir Alan Brooke—First Sea Lord and Chief of the Imperial General Staff, respectively—Patton was unimpressed, writing, "Brooke is nothing but a clerk" and "Pound slept most of the time." He saw them as unfit for their positions, writing, "The more I see of the so-called greats the less they impress me—I am better." According to Martin Blumenson, "Pound was already suffering the effects of a brain tumor, discovered somewhat later, and he would die that year." As it happened, Brooke was no more impressed with Patton, writing that he was "[a] real fire-eater and definitely a character." Similarly, Patton's encounter with British Vice Admiral Lord Louis Mountbatten left him with the distinct impression that the latter was "charming but not impressive. I think he got [i.e., learned] more from us [American military brass] than we got from him."

Patton was also fairly unimpressed with Churchill, who "speaks the worst French I have ever heard, his eyes run, and he is not at all impressive," though he later found that he "got on well" with Churchill and found him to be "cunning rather than brilliant but with great tenacity," although he was "easily flattered—all of them are." His encounters with Roosevelt, on the other hand, all left a good impression, as he wrote that FDR was "most affable and interested" and that they "got on fine," even noting, "He really appeared as a great statesman." Ironically, Patton's views on the two would later flip-flop, as he would side with Churchill against Roosevelt and his cronies in insisting that the Allies recognize the impending danger of the Soviet menace.

Though Patton's diary entries throughout the course of the conference reveal his disdain for politicians, two especially stand out. In the first, he recounted how Harry Hopkins, the secretary of commerce and one of Roosevelt's closest advisers, had asked him if he would be interested in becoming an ambassador. Patton told him that he "would resign and go fishing rather than take such a job." While other entries show that Patton actually did like Hopkins quite well, finding him to be intelligent and a good conversationalist, it was clear that Patton had nothing but disdain for diplomacy, a fact which would become increasingly clear throughout the course of the war. Second, on January 21, he recorded in his diary, "Millions of pictures were taken and none for the glory of the troops, all for the glory of FDR, and for Clark when he could get a chance. It was very disgusting."

Although Patton's disgust was likely focused most acutely on the fact that Clark, his rival, was getting glory and schmoozing with politicians, and though his other entries clearly indicate that he liked the president, Patton's entry here clearly demonstrates his disdain for nonmilitary professions and especially for the adulteration of military matters with politics. He was rather eager, however, to receive his second Distinguished Service Medal from Eisenhower, who also attended the conference. Eisenhower intimated to Patton that he was growing tired of Clark and that "he had suggested to Gen. Marshall that I [Patton] be made deputy commanding general AFHQ [Allied Forces Headquarters] and run the war while he [Eisenhower] runs the politics."

Oddly, Patton balked at the notion of being Ike's second-in-command, writing, "I doubt if it [the appointment] comes out and am not sure I want [the] job." Ultimately, Eisenhower decided against it, thereby freeing Patton of the decision as to whether or not he would accept such a promotion. Indeed, when he received the news that he would not become the theater commander in Tunisia, Patton wrote in his diary: "I think I was fortunate in not being made Deputy Commander-in-Chief to Ike. I guess destiny is still on the job. God, I wish I could really command and lead as well as just fight." It seems, then, that Patton was still eager for promotion, but not at the cost of serving on the front lines with his men.

Spirits were fairly high during the conference, since the arrival of American troops in the North African theater symbolized the turning of the tide in the struggle against Germany. Indeed, the Casablanca Conference itself proved to be a turning point in the prosecution of the war from a military standpoint. But it did not come without conflict, as the Anglo-American combined chiefs of staff butted heads debating strategy in what Carlo D'Este calls "the stormiest negotiations ever to occur between the two Allies."

Fortunately for Patton, he was not involved in these meetings and was thereby spared the internecine fighting over strategic aims. In the end, it was agreed that the Sicily campaign would be in the first position. Equally significant was the announcement by Roosevelt at the concluding press conference that the Allies would demand "unconditional surrender by Germany, Italy, and Japan. That means a reasonable assurance of future world peace. It does not mean the destruction of the population of Germany, Italy, or Japan, but it does mean the destruction of the philosophies in those countries which are based on conquest and the subjugation of other people."

There is some debate as to whether Churchill was surprised by Roosevelt's seemingly impromptu announcement. Either way, it seems Roosevelt made the decision, in part, to gratify Stalin, as he realized that the Soviet leader was growing impatient waiting for his allies to open the second front. Indeed, Stalin was pleased by the announcement, though he did his best to hide it. He knew that unconditional surrender would make the Germans more likely to hold out against them, thereby giving the Red Army more time to get to Berlin.

Three weeks before, the German commander in the south, Gen. Albert Kesselring, had put out feelers for a negotiated surrender, using SS Gen. Karl Wolff to make contact with Allen Dulles, the head of the Office of Strategic Services (OSS) in Berne, Switzerland. The Russians were informed of the approach, but as it seemed unlikely to lead to anything, they were not invited to take part in the initial, informal conversations. However, Stalin's paranoia was quickly aroused. He wrote to Roosevelt: "I cannot understand why the representatives of the Soviet Command have been excluded from the talks in [Berne]. In a situation of this kind allies should have nothing to conceal from each other." The Allies had, in fact, not concealed anything. In Moscow, Stalin told Gen. Zhukov, "This is some more proof of the backstage intrigues carried on between the Hitlerites and the British Government circles."

It would also guarantee that the Americans could not accept an earlier surrender as was offered, even up until the time the Americans were in Berlin.

Patton concerned himself primarily with the tactical side of warfare, an arrangement that suited him fine. However, as a battlefield general and a man of honor prepared to protect the women of his defeated foes, he would lament, "for the first week after the Russians took Berlin, all woman who ran were shot and those who did not were raped. I could have taken Berlin if I had been allowed." Inclined to avoid the more diplomatic aspects of leadership, Patton had little influence over the strategic decisions reached at the conference in Casablanca, a dynamic that left him with diminished control over his own destiny.

Thus, when it was agreed, as part of the Anglo-American strategic compromise, that subordination of theater operations would fall to British command, it was British Field Marshal Harold Alexander who would become Eisenhower's second-in-command, not Patton. While Patton was happy to have avoided becoming Ike's "number two," he was furious at the notion that American officers would have to submit to British command. He blustered, "We have sold our birthright," claiming the move had "Shades of J. J. Pershing" all over it, referring to Pershing's decision to allow French officers to command American troops in the summer of 1917. Aside from the decision to give the British authority over American soldiers, however, Patton did not voice any qualms he had about the decisions reached at Casablanca—at least for the time being. Later in the war, however, it became apparent that the decision to demand unconditional surrender handcuffed the Western Allies, allowing Stalin to continue pushing the Red Army through Central and Eastern Europe.

Tehran 1943

If the policy of "unconditional surrender" was the most significant outcome of the Casablanca conference, then the future of postwar Germany would be the uppermost topic of discussion later that year in Tehran.

While Churchill insisted upon a "moderate reorganization" of the German state, Stalin and Roosevelt both pushed for more complete dismemberment, in hopes of preventing a third world war. While in Tehran, FDR and Stalin met privately several times.

"For his part, Stalin had played Roosevelt impeccably," said Simon Berthon in *Warlords*. "At all times he behaved respectfully towards him, in marked contrast to the rudeness he often displayed to Churchill." During these discussions, Roosevelt played up disagreements between the British and American governments and invited the Soviets to participate in the postwar deconstruction of the French and British empires. Additionally, the president implied that he would respect Soviet control in Poland and the Baltic states.

Other major decisions at Tehran included agreement on the timing of the opening of the second front and Soviet involvement in the war against Japan within three months of the German surrender. When Roosevelt and Stalin overruled Churchill on when to open the second front, Roosevelt allegedly winked at the Soviet leader, indicating their increasingly tightening relationship. Behind the scenes, a generation of British soldiers had been killed. Churchill could not afford any more casualties.

Eisenhower also was hesitant to lose any more lives, the casualties already numbering in the hundreds of thousands. Thus, by his calculations, the Allies would need to allow Stalin to invade Berlin from the East with nothing short of a horde of millions. At times the limitations of resources and political will would also be the victim of Soviet aggression, not simply a battle of political wills.

In October 1944, Churchill flew to Moscow to meet with Stalin in a conference code named Tolstoy. The two leaders of the European Allies met under the assumption that the United States would return to its standard historical policy of isolationism in the wake of the war. As such, it seemed likely that the United States would not keep its troops on European soil for very long after the war had concluded, thereby leaving Great Britain and the Soviet Union to govern Europe. After some preliminary discussions regarding the future of Poland, in which it was decided that the British would pressure the Polish government-in-exile (then residing in London) to negotiate with the Soviet puppet government in Lublin, the two moved on to the question of the postwar order in Eastern Europe and the Balkans.

It was here that Churchill wrote what he referred to as a "naughty document"—later known as the "percentages agreement"—on a piece of scrap paper. He had just told Stalin that

> it was better to express these things in diplomatic terms
> and not to use the phrase "dividing into spheres," because
> the Americans might be shocked. But, he said, as long as
> he and Marshal Stalin understood each other he could
> explain matters to the president.

Unbeknownst to the British prime minister, Stalin had already foreseen the coming conflict with the Western powers; as he told Foreign Minister Vyacheslav Molotov in 1942, "The question of borders will be decided by force." But as early as 1912 he had made his purposes well known: "We think that a powerful and vigorous movement is impossible without differences—'true conformity' is possible only in the cemetery."

Churchill proposed that the Soviet Union ("Russia") and other countries divide up postwar influence over the Balkans and Eastern Europe by percentages. The proposal read as follows:

Romania: Russia 90%, the others 10%
Greece: Britain (in accord with USA) 90%, Russia 10%
Yugoslavia: 50/50%
Hungary: 50/50%
Bulgaria: Russia 75%, the others 25%

Stalin edited the "naughty document," changing the Soviets' share of Bulgaria to 90 percent and the "others'" share to 10 percent. He then signified his approval of the agreement with a check mark. "After this," Churchill later recalled,

there was a long pause. The penciled paper lay in the center of the table. At length I said, "Might it not be thought rather cynical if it seemed we had disposed of these issues, so fateful to millions of people, in such an offhand manner? Let us burn the paper." "No, you keep it," said Stalin.

The following day, discussions between Soviet Foreign Minister Vyacheslav Molotov and British Foreign Minister Anthony Eden continued along similar lines. These talks came to nothing, which was no surprise to Stalin, who, as Simon Sebag Montefiore writes, considered them "surely a bemusing attempt to negotiate what was already a fait accompli." Though ultimately the "naughty document" did not go into effect—Churchill and Stalin's joint cable to Roosevelt did not even mention that portion of their talks—it symbolized what was to come, as the Allies would soon effectively carve up Europe between themselves, thereby setting the course of global history for the coming decades.

Yalta 1945

The final meeting of the Big Three took place at Yalta in February 1945. In that coastal city on the shores of the Black Sea—which, due to the surrounding region's devastation at the hands of the Nazis, Churchill called "The Riviera of Hades"—Roosevelt, Churchill, and Stalin settled on a framework for governing postwar Europe. As historian John Lewis Gaddis observes, although "[t]he Yalta conference of February 1945 is usually considered the great decision-making conclave of the war," that conference "merely filled in the outline already sketched at Teheran."

By this point, Roosevelt had come to terms with Soviet strength and had worked to ensure their collaboration in the postwar world. He hoped to strike a balance between his commitment to the principle of self-determination and the need for Stalin's cooperation both to win the war and to establish a stable postwar order; perhaps "Uncle Joe" would permit a modicum of self-determination and the free flow of goods and information within the Soviet sphere of influence after the war. In case Stalin was unwilling to come to such an understanding, as George Herring recounts in *From Colony to Superpower*, Roosevelt "hedged his bets by refusing to share with the Soviet leader information about work on the atomic bomb—about which Stalin was already aware—and by holding back commitments of postwar economic aid."

The postwar framework to which the Big Three agreed effectively sealed the fate of Eastern and Western Europe—and, in a sense, that of the whole world—for decades to come. It was at Yalta that Roosevelt, Churchill, and Stalin finalized much of what had been discussed at Tehran regarding the future of Europe.

The most important decision reached at Yalta was that the Soviet Union would be given influence in Manchuria and other parts of China in exchange for its entry into the war against Japan following the defeat of Germany. Another crucial agreement was that Germany would be occupied and governed by an Allied coalition after the Red Army took Berlin. It was to be divided into American, British, French, and Russian zones. This was a tidy solution on paper but impractical in reality, considering the chasm that existed between Russian and Western cultures. Additionally, the Allies agreed that the states on the USSR's borders should be "friendly" toward the Soviets and that the Soviets would allow free elections in the territories they had liberated from the Nazis.

But what did the words *democracy* and *liberty* mean to a totalitarian dictator on one side and two constitutional democrats on the other? It was never spelled out. In only a few years' time, it became apparent that the decision to trust the Soviets in Eastern Europe had been a poor one and that Anglo-American forces should have pressed their advantage and taken Berlin. Patton had warned against allowing the Soviets to have their way, but his superiors ignored his warnings for the sake of their wartime alliance with Stalin.

Stalin was delighted, as reflected in a fictitious story he liked to tell after the war. In his anecdote, the Big Three went bear hunting. Once they had bagged a bear:

> Churchill said, "I'll take the bearskin. Let Roosevelt and Stalin divide the meat." Roosevelt said, "No, I'll take the skin. Let Churchill and Stalin divide the meat." Stalin remained quiet so Churchill and Roosevelt asked him: "Mister Stalin, what do you say?" Stalin simply replied, "The bear belongs to me—after all, I killed it."

In this parable, the bear represented Hitler, while the bearskin was a metaphor for Eastern Europe, and Stalin got it all.

The Antihero Loses Ground

As the war progressed and a cohesive grand strategy for its conclusion came into view, Patton's own star began to dim. More and more, his own sensibilities were in direct conflict with those of his superiors. Patton grew more irascible as the effort to block him escalated.

An unsettling example of the challenge to Patton's destiny was revealed in the waning days of the war, as the Allies, and most notably Patton's Third Army, moved into position, poised to take the strategic cities of Vienna, Prague, and Berlin. It was a tragic example of what might have been when, twice in the spring of 1945, Patton made fervent pleas to Eisenhower for approval to take the Eastern European capitals in an effort to hold the Russians at their original borders. Though originally part of the Allied war plan, this strategy was no longer acceptable to the Allied heads of state, due to conference agreements and Soviet advances. Both times Patton requested permission from Ike to push onward, he was ordered to stand down.

Patton made his first request on April 30, 1945. With Allied troops perched along the Berlin city limits, Eisenhower deferred to the Russians and diverted resources to southern Germany. Patton pleaded with Eisenhower, insisting that "we had better take Berlin, and quick—and on to the Oder!" to prevent Russian advances. "Patton persisted, arguing that Simpson's Ninth Army could be in Berlin within forty-eight hours!" Simpson agreed; he only had "sixty miles to go, and the war would end." Eisenhower, still refusing to acknowledge its importance, shockingly responded, but "who would want it?"

That question clearly defined the distinction between the roles of politician and fighting generals, and how they viewed the end of the war. In response, Patton placed both hands on Eisenhower's shoulders, saying, "I think history will answer that for you." Sadly, Patton's words proved prophetic. That night, Patton heard on the radio that Roosevelt had died, and while the body of the president who had led the United States during the war was paraded down the streets of Washington, the Russians continued their creep west to play out their role as the U.S. ally of convenience.

Eisenhower did not suspect (or perhaps did not want to know) that what Stalin said publicly was not what he said privately. All along, Stalin was aware that Berlin was the crown jewel, essential to a future reign over Europe. Stalin innocently responded to Eisenhower's decision, saying: "Your plans completely coincide with the plans of the Red Army. Berlin has lost its former strategic importance. The Soviet High Command therefore plans to allow secondary forces in the direction of Berlin." But to his astounded commanders Stalin asked, "Well, then, who is going to take Berlin: are we or the Allies?"

With the Allies tired and focused on another theater of operations besides Europe, the Russians took advantage of their good fortune and energetically moved in. Eisenhower informed Patton that Berlin would be taken by neither the American nor the British Army but by the Red Army. Patton was shocked, disgusted, and dispirited by the news.

Stalin had not only lied to Eisenhower but also had convinced him that Berlin was an empty military symbol, one not worth fighting for, when the war was practically won. As Cold War historian Paul Kengor reflects:

Western Europe won the peace, Eastern Europe did not. And imagine if you lived in Czechoslovakia or East Berlin or Poland. Those people, their reward for the defeat of the Nazis at the end of World War Two was another four and a half decades of totalitarian occupation, this time under the Soviets.

Deals with the Devil

How did Patton's war come to this? Why was he forced to sit idly by and wait for the Red Army to take Berlin when he was within easy striking distance? Why did the Allies spend years spilling the blood of thousands of men to oust a dictator in Germany and recapture the land from the German Reich only to surrender those liberated lands to a Russian tyrant in a matter of months?

The answer, in a word, was diplomacy.

Historians still debate and ponder the questions of that decision and how it has resonated throughout the decades. Former U.S. Secretary of State Henry Kissinger, with his real-world experience, wrote in his seminal Cold War memoir *Diplomacy*:

> Was an alternate strategy feasible? Or were the democracies doing the best they could, given the geographic and military realities that existed at the time? These are haunting questions, because in retrospect, everything that happened seems inevitable. The longer the interval, the more difficult it becomes to imagine an alternative outcome or to prove its viability. And history refused to be played back like a movie reel in which new endings are spliced into at will.

In the end, Eisenhower demurred to diplomacy. He stepped back military from Berlin for three reasons: the Yalta Agreement, battle exhaustion, and his perception of Berlin as lacking strategic significance.

At Yalta, a wary Churchill and an ill and weakened Roosevelt gave the Soviets rights in Berlin. The agreement provided a mechanism for dividing the city into four quadrants and allowed the Russians to enter Berlin while the American and British forces stood idly by creating long-lasting chaos and tragedy.

Likewise, the fatigue of war was real, but many, including Patton, believe the cost of taking Berlin was manageable. Montgomery and Patton, two seasoned military leaders could have reached Berlin within days of one another. German resistance would have been weaker for the Anglo-American force because the German people believed the grounds of their surrender would not be as onerous as surrender to the Russians would be. American historian Michael Beschloss reminds us: "Almost 70 American divisions [between 10,000 and 20,000 men] had rushed into Germany faster than the Red Army, which often moved on foot and by primitive horse-drawn vehicles. American forces had thrust 150 miles into the Soviet occupation zone. Many Germans, afraid of the Soviets and their armies, were straining to surrender to the Americans."

Finally Eisenhower believed, Berlin was merely symbolic, and that controlling the German capital was not critical to the geo-political situation. On this point, Eisenhower was sorely wrong. Far from insignificant, Berlin would remain at the heart of the conflict for the duration of the Cold War. As David Clay Large, author of *Berlin*, writes:

> Berlin became the most dangerous flash point of the Cold War. Its importance, early on, was strategic. If the Soviets could force their former allies to evacuate Berlin, demoralization and a sense of abandonment by the U.S. might spread over Western Europe. They might have achieved a principal goal: a unified, demilitarized, and politically

nonaligned Germany—which, no doubt, would eventually drop into the communist camp.

Berlin, which had been the vibrant, liberal cultural center of Germany until the ascension of Nazism in 1933, had a real chance at a democratic future. But Eisenhower allowed the Soviets to gain a strategic foothold that could have easily gone to the Americans. Antony Beevor explains: "Militarily, it might have been feasible for Eisenhower's forces to reach Hitler's capital before the Red Army, but such an advance would have precipitated a clash between the Allies. The Russians would have been outraged by any attempt to deprive them of their prize."

If Eisenhower was ambivalent about the strategic importance of Berlin, Stalin was clear-eyed about its necessity to the Soviet future.He saw Berlin as the stronghold from which to rule all of Eastern Europe and to divide the West. And divide he would. As Beevor wrote, Stalin captured Berlin in part to "tak[e] it from Hitler, but partly also [to] ensur[e] its denial to Roosevelt and Churchill." Furthermore, Stalin knew the Germans were racing to develop nuclear weapons under the direction of Werner Heisenberg at the Kaiser Wilhelm Institute for Physics. Soviet scientists who had studied at the Institute were aware that Heisenberg's colleagues not only knew how to split the atom but were also creating a nuclear reactor. When the troops took Berlin, Lavrenty Beria, head of the NKVD, sent his secret service men to take the institute before the Americans arrived. Three tons of uranium oxide, which would have given the Soviets enough to start working on their own atomic weapons, were allegedly captured. It is estimated that such a cache would give them a 10-year advantage over the United States. The arms race was on.

The question remains: Was the United States really so blind to Stalin's motives that it opened the door to the tragedies in Eastern Europe that followed? Again, Beevor offers an excellent response:

The basic problem . . . was that the Americans at that
stage simply did not view Europe in strategic terms. They
had a simple and limited objective: to win the war against
Germany quickly, with as few casualties as possible, and
then concentrate on Japan. Eisenhower—like his president, the chiefs of staff, and other senior officials—failed
to look ahead and completely misread Stalin's character.

Some British officers even referred to Eisenhower's
deference to Stalin as "Have a Go, Joe," a call used by
British prostitutes when soliciting American soldiers.

In Berlin, Patton was not advocating for a third world war; he
merely wanted to push the Russian army back to its original borders. He was no statesmen, but he knew his military history and recognized the Russian empire emerging from the rubble of a British
Empire no longer able to hide behind its bulwark in Germany.
The emerging empire behaved in a way Harvard historian Graham
Allison would argue could be seen in 500 years of modern history
and even dating back to the ancient. Stalin says it best, "Everyone
imposes his own system as far as his army can reach," and Allison
would later call this phenomenon the "Thucydides Trap," from
The History of the Peloponnesian Wars: "Thucydides's Trap refers to
the natural, inevitable discombobulation that occurs when a rising
power threatens to displace a ruling power."

Patton knew from history that Sparta would fear the expansion
of Athenian power and face an inevitable clash. Thucydides would
write that the entire Peloponnesian War was due to "the growth
in power of Athens, and the alarm which this inspired in Sparta."
Allison, in his *Destined for War*, affirms this loss of political will that
could encroach on the needed: "When states repeatedly fail to act
in what appears to be their true national interest, it is often because
their policies reflect necessary compromises among parties within

their government rather than a single coherent vision." He adds, "The German philosopher Nietzsche taught us that the most common form of human stupidity is forgetting what one is trying to do."

In Patton's case, the answer was to win the war, and to his mind, that included both Western and Eastern Europe. That meant not understanding but confronting the Russians. He would write:

> From what I have seen of them I have no particular desire to understand them except to ascertain how much lead or iron it takes to kill them. In addition to his other amiable characteristics, the Russians have no regard for human life and they are all out sons of bitches, barbarians and chronic drunks. If it should be necessary for us fight the Russians. the sooner we do it the better.

At the dawn of the Cold War, the general's foul words and prescient voice were not welcome. It was more convenient to gag Patton. It might have been the final wartime chance to stop the Red Menace from bleeding into Eastern Europe and constructing a wall. As historian Paul Kengor laments, in the end:

> Not only did the Soviets take Eastern Europe for 44 years, but all these great, wondrous, ancient and old cities and territories fell behind the Iron Curtain. They had no freedom of the press, no freedom of speech, no freedom of assembly, no freedom of religion. They don't even have the right to emigrate. And they build a wall to keep people from leaving. If you try to go over the wall that has barbed wire on it, your own people, your own police shoot you.

Patton knew Berlin had always been the crown jewel of Europe, in much the same way Sicily had been to Greece and Rome in the ancient world. Berlin held the key to the Soviet Union's future, and Stalin did not hesitate. As Henry Kissinger later wrote: "Contravening his assurances to Eisenhower, he [Stalin] ordered the main thrust of the Soviet ground offensive to be aimed at Berlin, giving Marshals Zhukov and Konev two weeks to launch an attack he had told Eisenhower would not take place until the second half of May!" Patton thought this was not only the wrongful intervention of politics but a lack of national will. The same malaise that Gibbon in his *Decline and Fall of the Roman Empire* had determined as a symptom of the end of empire, Patton ascribed to the conclusion of World War II: "[we] forgot that the best of omens is to unsheathe our sword in the defence of our country."

In the end, Patton lamented, "I could have taken Berlin had I been allowed."

....

CHAPTER SIX

Cold War on the Horizon

As the world would soon conclude, the agreements at Tehran and Yalta sowed the seeds of the geopolitical contest that would roil the world for the next 50 years. For Patton, the framework created by the Big Three at Casablanca, Tehran, and Yalta, and the military decisions that would follow, belied the collective and sacred duty as he understood it to save Western civilization. Surely, American soldiers and Allied forces had not attended to the war in Europe simply to trade one tyrant for another—or as the Poles understood, the "two faces of evil."

Patton's opinion at this point would be dismissed, though he concurred with Churchill, who said, "Germany is finished. Though it may take some time to clean up the mess, the real problem is Russia. I can't get the Americans to see it."

By 1945, the winds of war had shifted, and they were not blowing in Patton's favor. The qualities that had made Patton the right man at the right time at the beginning of the war were now viewed as a hindrance at its conclusion. Indeed, his abrasive and dogged leadership, his singularity of purpose, and his relentless pursuit of victory would ultimately land him behind a desk in a backwater of postwar Germany. But before being relegated to an inauspicious administrative role, Patton would hold nothing back in a final heroic effort to save Eastern Europe from what he instinctively knew would be an even more menacing regime.

Just days after being redirected away from Berlin in the spring of 1945, Patton's Third Army was rapidly approaching the Czechoslovakian capital. He witnessed the brave efforts of the Czechoslovak Resistance against the Nazi occupation and wanted to help them wrest control of their country back from the Germans. To him, the objective was far-reaching, simple and clear: Push forward as fast and as far as the Third Army could go until it met the Red Army, thereby stopping the Soviet advance. This broad sweep would take Patton deep into Czechoslovakia and Austria and would give the West control of the greater part of the European heartland, the geopolitical pivot of the continent. What to Patton was obvious, however, became an Achilles heel for the rest of the Allied command, now obligated to honoring an unsavory bargain.

Stalin's Designs

For Stalin, who once said, "The death of one man is a tragedy, the death of millions is a statistic," ridding Eastern Europe of its German occupiers was not about freedom, but future world domination. Indeed, this had been Stalin's plan since before the war began. As historian Richard Pipes writes, given the failed Soviet efforts to "export revolution" to Europe after the Russian Revolution and the USSR's abortive campaign into Poland in 1919–1921, Stalin believed "that the best hope for spreading [his] regime was to promote another world war." Thus, for much of the interwar period, the Red Army secretly cooperated with the German military, allowing them to manufacture and test weapons on Russian territory, thereby enabling the Germans to secretly violate the disarmament provisions of the Treaty of Versailles.

Stalin's strategy also led to the infamous Molotov-Ribbentrop Pact (August 1939) between the Soviet Union and Nazi Germany, a nonaggression pact with a secret clause regarding the division of Poland between the two powers. In Stalin's mind, the war would largely play out in the West, leaving Eastern and Central Europe open for the Soviets to sweep through.

While true that Stalin continuously ignored warnings by both his own intelligence services and the Allies that the Germans were preparing to invade the Soviet Union in Operation Barbarossa, he had known that two countries predicated on Communism and Nazism could not cooperate interminably. Indeed, they were polar opposites and were all but destined to clash. This is perhaps best demonstrated by the fact that Stalin harbored no ill-will against Foreign Minister Molotov in the wake of the German invasion in June 1941. Stalin had simply thought that with the capitalist powers fighting it out in the West, the Soviet Union could wait and build its strength before engaging Germany in a war; he saw the war in Western Europe as a means of wearing down his capitalist foes, in a strategy that international relations expert John J. Mearsheimer calls "bloodletting."

As historian Georg von Rauch notes, "The alliance with the Western powers from 1941 on must not blind us to the fact that for the Bolsheviks the war which began in 1939 represented the long hoped-for conflict among the capitalist states which could become the springboard for world revolution." Thus, as World War II ended, Stalin saw that he could finally realize his prewar goals of spreading Soviet communism in Europe; indeed, his wartime deals with Roosevelt regarding Asia and the activity of the Communist Party USA indicate that he was equally eager to spread his ideology to other continents as well.

Prague Bleeding

In early May 1945, as the Allies shut down the Nazi war machine, Patton stood with his massive Third Army on the outskirts of Prague in a potential face-off with the Red Army. He pleaded for Gen. Eisenhower's green light to advance and capture the city for the Allies, which also would have meant containment of the Russians. British Prime Minister Churchill also thought the move crucial and beneficial for postwar Europe and insisted upon it, but to no avail. Eisenhower denied Patton's request, and the Russians took the region, which would pay dearly for years to come. The destiny of millions was reduced to mass starvation, blood revenge, and distant gulags. At the time, Patton understood the tragedy of this event and wrote: "We promised the Europeans freedom. It would be worse than dishonorable not to see that they have it. This might mean war with the Russians, but what of it?"

But once again, with an opportunity to "win the peace" within reach, Eisenhower ordered Patton to stand down. Ike made this decision despite the fact that Churchill, the British Imperial Chiefs of Staff, and the U.S. State Department had all advocated for the Americans to continue their advance and capture Prague before the Red Army could beat them to it. Though Eisenhower allowed Patton's Third Army to enter Czechoslovakia on May 4, he ordered them not to advance past Pilsen. In his diary on May 6, a bitter Patton wrote:

> The halt line through Pilsen is mandatory. . . . Eisenhower
> does not wish at this late date to have any international
> complications. It seems to me that as great a nation as
> America should let the other people worry about the
> complications. Personally, I would go to the line of
> the Moldau River and tell the Russians that is where I
> intended to stop.

Patton, fuming, called Eisenhower to demand an explanation. Ike explained that he had agreed to the halt in discussions with Soviet Gen. Aleksei Antonov, as the two commanders wanted to avoid any potential problems that might result from American and Soviet forces meeting. But as Jonathan Jordan notes: "The Red Army was nowhere near Prague. He [Patton] could have gone further and there would have been no danger of blue-on-blue or friendly fire [between the Americans and the Russians] at that point." Worse still, the decision to cede Prague to the Soviets underscored perceived Western complacence regarding Czechoslovakia, first demonstrated by the infamous Munich Agreement of 1938, in which then British Prime Minister Neville Chamberlain agreed to let Hitler invade the sovereign nation.

Learning of the American advance into Czechoslovakia, the people of Prague rose up against the Germans, having heard a false report that the Third Army was within 20 miles of the city. Unfortunately, seizure of the radio station in Prague by Czechoslovak partisans had led to confusion on the part of the German occupiers, who were inclined to discredit reports of the war's end and continue fighting. Therefore, although the war had officially ended, Prague was still in danger from the German forces near that city. Patton was briefed by a team of personnel from the Office of Strategic Services, or OSS, the precursor to the CIA, who informed him of the catastrophe. He begged Bradley to allow him to advance to Prague to help the partisans, but Bradley refused, as he had no desire to contradict Eisenhower's halt order.

On the morning of May 7, Czechoslovakian representatives asked for aid, not only so they could take their capital back from the Germans but—just as important—so they could recapture it before the Red Army arrived. They also requested that Czechoslovak forces, then with Bradley's army group, be sent into Prague. Czechoslovak appeals were also made directly to Patton, whose forces were near

Pilsen; it would have been easy for him to make a rapid advance eastward to aid the Czechoslovaks in their struggle. This word reached Col. Anthony J. Drexel Biddle, Jr., of Allied Force Headquarters, on the morning of May 7. He naturally said that Prague was included in the terms of surrender and that hostilities had ended.

More desperate appeals came from the Czechoslovaks on May 7 and 8, now directly to Prime Minister Churchill, begging him to do something or to take up the matter directly with the U.S. government. Churchill urgently wired Eisenhower, suggesting that Allied forces could enter Prague ahead of the Russians, but Eisenhower did not approve such action. That day, he accepted the formal surrender of Germany at his headquarters at Rheims, France. Eisenhower continued to honor Antonov's request of May 5 that the American forces remain west of the Pilsen-Karlsbad line, while keeping the Russians informed of Czechoslovakian pleas for aid.

On May 8, the Czechoslovaks asked for bombers to be sent to defend Prague, but Supreme Headquarters naïvely forwarded the message to Moscow with the comment that no action was being taken. Sadly, on the same day, the Czechoslovaks were notified that Allied forces had stopped at the request of the Russians and that all appeals for help should now go to the Red Army. Prague's patriotic citizens, it seemed, were doomed to the same fate as their counterparts in the Warsaw Uprising of August 1944, when the Polish Underground had risen up and attacked their German occupiers, in hopes of reclaiming their city before the Red Army, which had been just miles away, arrived. The uprising failed, however, and while the Red Army's advance was halted on the city limits because it outran its supply lines, Stalin would not permit American bombers to aid the Polish insurgents, thereby effectively allowing the Germans to do the dirty work for him before his army took the city. Stalin was quite familiar with such a scenario and was willing to take full advantage of it.

The Red Army entered Prague on May 12, almost a week after Patton had pleaded with Eisenhower to let him capture the city. It is in these moments of mounting tension between military strategy and foreign policy that clashes occur, and Patton finally drew a line in the sand. Recognizing that the Red Army now posed an equal or greater threat than the once-great Nazi war machine, Patton pushed back against Supreme Headquarters. He admonished Undersecretary of War Robert Patterson, saying:

> Let's keep our boots polished, bayonets sharpened, and present a picture of force and strength to these people [the Russians]. This is the only language they understand and respect. If you fail to do this, then I would like to say to you that we have had a victory over the Germans and have disarmed them, but have lost the war. . . . Let's not give them [the Russians] time to build up their supplies. If we do, then I repeat, we have had a victory over the Germans and disarmed them; we have failed in the liberation of Europe; we have lost the war!

Later, Patton wrote of the decision not to take Prague: "I was very much chagrined, because I felt, and still feel, that we should have gone on the Moldau River and, if the Russians didn't like it, let them go to hell."

Patton's warnings were to no avail. The Allied troops were forced to hold steady just short of full, lasting victory. Meanwhile, the Red Army continued its westward surge, killing not only the remaining Nazi forces but the anti-Nazi resistance groups as well, thereby all but ensuring Soviet dominance of the postwar politics in those countries.

Even before the war, Stalin had become accustomed to the use of force as a means to political ends, as seen in his Great Purge (or Great

Terror) of the 1930s, during which he jailed millions of dissidents and even loyal communists whom he had perceived as a threat to his power, and had hundreds of thousands of those prisoners executed, often without a trial. For Stalin, in the words of Russian poet Osip Mandelstam, "every killing is a treat." Indeed, over the course of his rule, Stalin killed tens of millions more people than Hitler did. Murdering a few thousand potential future dissidents in Eastern Europe was just good politics, nothing more and nothing less.

Stalin's view was a combination of both the antisemitism of the Allies and the Nazi view of race (from *Report* on January 26, 1934):

> Still others think that war should be organized by a "superior race," say, the German "race," against an "inferior race," primarily against the Slavs; that only such a war can provide a way out of the situation, for it is the mission of the "superior race" to render the "inferior race" fruitful and to rule over it. Let us assume that this queer theory, which is as far removed from science as the sky from the earth, let us assume that this queer theory is put into practice. What may be the result of that? It is well known that ancient Rome looked upon the ancestors of the present-day Germans and French in the same way as the representatives of the "superior race" now look upon the Slav races. It is well known that ancient Rome treated them as an "inferior race," as "barbarians," destined to live in eternal subordination to the "superior race," to "great Rome," and, between ourselves be it said, ancient Rome had some grounds for this, which cannot be said of the representatives of the "superior race" of today. (Thunderous applause.) But what was the upshot of this? The upshot was that the non-Romans, i.e., all the "barbarians," united against the common enemy and brought Rome down with a crash. The

question arises: What guarantee is there that the claims
of the representatives of the "superior race" of today will
not lead to the same lamentable results? What guarantee
is there that the fascist literary politicians in Berlin will be
more fortunate than the old and experienced conquerors
in Rome? Would it not be more correct to assume that the
opposite will be the case?

So, despite general awareness about Stalin's violent nature and
his schemes for domination, Eastern Europe was handed to him on
a silver platter, for a long-awaited vision of world dominance. His
immediate steps would be to keep a low profile and wait out the
American retreat from Europe. All the while, Patton had warned
against such action, and although he was in agreement with Prime
Minister Churchill and the people of Prague itself, his voice faded.
And with his prophetic muting came an invitation to a Cold War.

Sounding the Alarm

Patton was deeply affected by Eisenhower's decisions to hold back
from entering both Berlin and Prague. When ordered to stand down,
perhaps Patton could hear the cries of the millions who would never
know freedom but would certainly know death. Though much
more of a tactician than a strategist, Patton recognized the historical
importance of allowing the Soviets to conquer Eastern and Central
Europe. Indeed, Patton expert Charles Province puts it well when
he says that with Eisenhower's decision not to liberate Prague, "we
lost the Cold War right then and there."

To Patton's sensibilities, the foreign policy decisions forged by
the Big Three at Yalta contradicted the Allied mission, and he was
not timid in voicing his opposition. He would have stood in the
shadows of Robert E. Lee's idea that: "[t]rue patriotism sometimes

requires of men to act exactly contrary, at one period, to that which it does at another, and the motive which impels them the desire to do right is precisely the same." Here was a case where the soldier in Patton was warring with his political statesman.

He also still harbored resentment toward Eisenhower and other members of the military hierarchy for strategic decisions they made during the war. When Ike hosted Patton and several other American commanders at lunch on May 10, Eisenhower "talked to us very confidentially on the necessity for solidarity in the event that any of us are called before a Congressional Committee," followed by "a speech which had to me the symptoms of political aspirations, on cooperation with the British, Russians, and the Chinese." To Patton, it seemed that

> this talking cooperation is for the purpose of covering up probable criticism of strategical blunders which he [Eisenhower] unquestionably committed during the campaign. Whether these were his own or due to too much cooperation with the British, I don't know. I am inclined to think he over-cooperated.

Clearly, Ike was concerned about his reputation, not least because, in Patton's accurate estimate, he was preparing for a post-war political career. As such, he wanted to eliminate any potential problems regarding the conduct of both the war and the occupation. Patton was less circumspect. In the coming days and weeks, he privately proposed to his military colleagues that Britain and America should now engage a defeated Germany as an ally against the Soviet Union. His thoughts echoed the earlier warnings of Churchill.

Patton's disdain for the Russians grew as the war's end approached. Following a visit from the commander of the 4th Guards Army, Gen. Nikanor Zakhvatayev, and other Russian military officers in May 1945, Patton noted in his diary, "I felt it was more correct for him to call on me than for me to call on him," indicating his low view of the Russian commander, despite the fact that Patton awarded him the Legion of Merit. After the awards ceremony, Patton and Zakhvatayev's party celebrated with American whiskey, which Patton noted they drank "without water with very bad results," and, as he boasted, Patton "unquestionably drank the Russian commander under the table and walked out under my own steam." The next day, Patton again outlasted his Russian guests by insisting that they drink whiskey instead of vodka, with the same results as the day before. Following that encounter, he recorded in his diary that he felt that the Russians "are a scurvy race and simply savages. We could beat hell out of them."

On May 14, Patton attended a banquet given in his honor by Soviet Marshal Fyodor I. Tolbukhin at a palace in Austria. Patton and his entourage had prepared for the heavy drinking at the banquet by "drinking two ounces of mineral oil before starting on the expedition" and being "very careful of what we drank." Despite the lavishness of the banquet, Patton's low opinion of the Soviets was evident in his diary entry that night, in which he wrote, "The officers with few exceptions give the appearance of recently civilized Mongolian bandits," and that the Soviets "give me the impression of something that is to be feared in future world political reorganization." Describing the event to a friend, Patton said that when the Russians had become too drunk to stand, he and his entourage shouldn't have stopped: "We should have gone on and taken those Russians. They're out to conquer the world!" The same day that he learned of the Japanese surrender, Patton wrote in his diary, "Well the war is over. . . . Now the horrors of peace, pacafism [sic] and unions will have unlimited sway. I wish I were young enough to fight in the next one. It would be . . . [great] killing Mongols."

Clearly, there was no love lost between Patton and the Russians. At the close of the war, he was one of the first to understand the geopolitical importance of keeping a buffer between the West and the Soviet Union. For decades, Germany had been that buffer. He knew that the Germans had spy networks in place and that they knew the terrain better than anyone else. He boldly stated:

> In my opinion and that of most nonpolitical officers, it is vitally necessary for us to build Germany up now as a buffer state against Russia. In fact, I am afraid we have waited too long. If we let Germany and the German people be completely disintegrated and starved, they will certainly fall for Communism and the fall of Germany for Communism will write the epitaph of Democracy in the United States.

Furthermore, Patton believed the decision to divide postwar Germany was unconscionable and short-sighted, a move he knew would feed Eastern Europe to the Russian Bear. He wrote:

> Russia knows what she wants and is laying her plans accordingly. We, on the other hand, and England and France to a lesser extent, don't know what we want and get less than nothing as a result. . . . Under the present system all that has been produced is a hot bed of anarchy and hopelessness which is ideal germinating ground for Communism.

"Uncle Joe"

Patton's contempt for Stalin and the Russians was more than a gut instinct. There was much available evidence to vindicate his assessment of the Russian leader and the brutality of the Red Army. The massacre of tens of thousands of Polish nationals in the Katyn Forest in 1940, for example, was widely believed to have happened at the hands of the NKVD, which would go on to kill between 50 million and 60 million people during Stalin's reign, many more than Adolf Hitler's SS killed. Yet Roosevelt (expediently) and Churchill (reluctantly) had accepted Stalin's adamant claim that the atrocities had come at the hand of the Nazis, a claim later proven false. Other Soviet conduct during the war, such as Stalin's handling of the Warsaw Uprising, also supported Patton's stern appraisal of the "Red Tsar." Later in the war, Russian trophy brigades looted and pillaged German cities and towns; one eyewitness reported "primal violence shattering all the restraining bonds of discipline. Almost all the buildings are burning. It is dark from smoke and soot. Walls are collapsing, crushing people."

Western historians would later estimate that at least two million German women were raped by Soviet soldiers, many of them repeatedly. When told of the Red Army's rampant sexual violence against both German and Russian women (many of the latter just freed from Nazi camps), Stalin purportedly told Yugoslavian President Milovan Djilas:

> You have of course read Dostoevsky? Do you see what a complicated thing is man's soul . . . ? Well then, imagine a man who has fought from Stalingrad to Belgrade—over thousands of kilometres of his own devastated land, across the dead bodies of his comrades and dearest ones? How can such a man react normally? And what is so awful about having his fun with a woman after such horrors?"

Patton recognized the Soviet penchant for being ruthless and unprincipled in waging war, as they punished both soldier and civilian alike.

Author of *Patton and Rommel, Men of War in the Twentieth Century*, Dennis Showalter adds: "The word Sadism is something that would come into Patton's mind. Because I think what he saw was the post war violent displacements. It was sadism. It had nothing to do with his concept of making war. And was his concept of how a man of war behaves." Victor Davis Hanson adds, "When we look back at it, it seems tragic, people were being killed right when Patton could've saved them, but he was fighting geo strategic currents that were so large and so vast." Patton wrote, "General Anders of the Polish 2 Corps told me that if his corps got between a German Army and a Russian Army he would have trouble deciding which direction to fight."

Of course, Churchill woul eventually draw public attention to the new Russian threat of which Patton had warned: "An iron curtain is drawn down upon their front. We do not know what is going on behind," but someday soon, as Patton predicted, they would "wreck Europe." By then, however, it was too late, with the fate of millions having been determined by the agreements at Yalta and later at Potsdam. Shortly after FDR's sudden death, newly minted President Harry S. Truman met with Stalin and newly elected British Prime Minister Clement Attlee at Potsdam, just outside Berlin. Truman, an avid poker player, was more willing than FDR to play hardball with the Soviet general secretary and wasted no time pandering to Stalin, to whom he politely whispered, "We have a new bomb." In the end, only by the force of the atomic bomb did Truman keep Stalin in check and gain his assurance for help against the Japanese in the Pacific. Despite this, the proverbial clock was ticking and, soon, the Cold War became reality, as Patton's warnings were ignored once more.

Little did Patton know that he would be unable to participate in the coming struggle between the superpowers. His brash, outspoken nature soon landed him in trouble once again. Patton's days were numbered. Instead of commanding a team on the battlefield, he would lead a team in the record room documenting the war.

....

CHAPTER SEVEN

A Desk Job

A wise king once wrote: "Vanities of vanities! All is vanity. What does man gain by all the toil at which he toils under the sun?" For Patton, the self-styled military hero devoted and glorious in battle, the war's end must have evoked a similar futile sentiment. In the final ignoble chapter of his storied career, Patton plays not only the antihero but also the tragic antihero. Relegated to an administrative position by Eisenhower, Patton would spend his final days not as a battlefield general but as general of Army records. The *genius* of war would conclude his service as *chronicler* of war.

Why a desk job? Some might conclude that Eisenhower was appeasing or even rewarding Patton by appealing to his intellect. More likely, he needed a quiet corner in which to deposit the increasingly vocal and contrary general. Patton's endearing traits, which might have been valued at the beginning of the war as fresh and innovative, were, by the end of the war, simply regarded as antagonistic, rebellious . . . even dangerous.

Out of Sight, Out of Mind

Two weeks after Germany surrendered, Gen. Eisenhower convened the high command in Europe in a conference room for lunch. Ike sent all of his commanders out of the room, leaving only the high command. He informed them that there would be a congressional investigation. Congress, he said, was going to be looking for mistakes that were made in this war, and it was crucial they present a united front to them and the American public. This would make everyone cautious about how they handled the press and their star general.

In late April 1945, Patton sensed the war in Europe was "sort of petering out." Even so, he seemed convinced he and his Third Army would soon be joining the war in the Pacific, and he wrote to his son George on April 28, "If you succeed in graduating a year from now, you will be able to join the Third Army in China." Little did he know that the order for American troops to occupy Germany, code-named Operation Eclipse, had already been formalized. The orders, dated April 25, outlined the necessity of American occupying forces in Germany. Though the formal appointment wouldn't come until July 1945, Patton was selected to serve as military governor of Bavaria, but not if he could help it.

Reticent to take on the largely civilian (and thus, for him, boring) work of being military governor of Bavaria, Patton begged Marshall to send him to fight in the Pacific theater. The Army chief of staff refused, largely because of Gen. Douglas MacArthur's penchant for, as Martin Blumenson puts it, "jealously guarding the publicity for himself, preferr[ing] a less colorful subordinate, not a prima donna like Patton." Beginning on June 4, Patton was sent on a month-long leave, first to Paris and London and then to the United States. The intent was both a bond-selling tour and a break for the veteran commander. Patton wrote that he looked forward to it "with no pleasure at all." His break from leading over a half-million men was anything but calm. Far from a quiet respite for a war-weary soldier, Patton was swarmed with well-wishers, supporters, fans, and wishful lovers at every stop. Citizens flocked to hear his scheduled speeches and learn, firsthand, of the exploits of Gen. Patton and his mighty Third Army. If he had kept his rhetoric in reserve and spoken only of past battlefields, he might have been safe, but safety was never a concern of Patton's. In his inimitable fashion, he spoke honestly, passionately, and with a candor that, in small doses, could be refreshing from normally stoic military brass. But his brutal, often tactless honesty about what war and soldiers were really like was not welcome on the home front.

During his leave, Patton gave several speeches, and some of them were met with great criticism from the American public. For instance, in a speech at the Hatch Memorial Shell in Boston, Patton was joined by almost 400 wounded veterans of the Third Army. He said: "It is a popular idea that a man is a hero just because he was killed in action. Rather, I think, a man is frequently a fool when he gets killed." Though Patton then proceeded to gesture to the wounded soldiers in the audience and say, "These men are the heroes," the press took his words out of context, making it sound as if he had no remorse for the loss of men under his command. Within the context of the evening and his preceding remarks, his statement had a radically different meaning than that solitary quote conveys. The facts are, even to this day many of us readily, rightfully, and without question praise the triumphant dead. We make memorials to their sacrifice and lionize their lives, but those veterans who stood shoulder to shoulder with them, the soldiers who came back from war scarred, mutilated, and seared, are often ignored and dismissed. Patton recognized it was far easier for civilians to honor the dead than it was to honor the living. The living are complicated, while the dead are not. He wanted all to know that his boys, the ones who came home without arms, legs, or worse, were just as much heroes as those who came back draped in their nation's flag. Yet, then, as it is today, nuance is not the hallmark of the press. As soon as that quote hit the stands, the shit hit the fan.

Gold Star mothers decried the general and wrote to all of Patton's superior officers in droves to voice their displeasure. The perception being pedaled was that Patton was a soulless brute, without a care for the men who died for his glory. Despite how discordant this view was with reality, it was embraced by the media. The reality was far different, as Patton broke down crying on several occasions, both when speaking of the men who had perished while under his command and while visiting soldiers who had been wounded while he had been their leader. At Walter Reed Hospital, he wept while visiting the double-amputation ward, saying, "God damn it, if I had been a better general, most of you wouldn't be here." It is difficult to say why the media was so merciless with Patton. Perhaps the prospect of peace meant that reporters needed a new villain to sell papers. Patton was already in their crosshairs following the slapping incidents, and his candor ensured that all they needed to do was follow Patton long enough and he would inevitably make headlines.

Marshall had directly instructed Patton to be careful in what he said while on leave in the United States, and Patton's numerous indiscretions did not go unnoticed. With complaints flooding into the War Department, Secretary Henry L. Stimson coached Patton on what he could and could not say. At a June 14 press conference, as Carlo D'Este recounts, Stimson personally led the meeting and so monopolized the microphone that Patton's only comments were "confined to innocuous but colorful and quotable lines about the Germans and his beloved Third Army." The general chaffed under Stimson's well-meaning instruction and thought that he was simply being "muzzled" once more. By the time he returned to Europe, Patton was relieved not only to have escaped from the direct gaze of the American public but also in a deeper way. He wrote in his diary:

> None of them [Americans] realizes that one cannot fight for
> two and a half years and be the same. Yet you are expected
> to get back into the identical groove from which you
> departed and from which your non-warlike compatriots
> have never moved.

Patton was, in this respect, equal to every soldier who has returned home from combat to find that the country they fought so hard to defend was utterly alien to them. Patton was overjoyed by every moment he had with his children, but America and he were now and forever on differing paths.

A Defiant Governor

Though Patton was bookish and well versed in military history, and he might have enjoyed his new role had it not been a demotion, he was not suited to administrative work. His aggressive personality served him well in war, but proved to be a handicap during peacetime.

Following Patton's domestic missteps, many wondered why a greater effort wasn't made to move Patton to a position better suited to his talents. Both Eisenhower and Marshall had deep reservations about him serving as governor of Bavaria. While it's true that MacArthur would not let Patton join the Pacific campaign under any circumstances, there were other options. Patton made it clear that his only passion beyond battle was teaching. They could have reassigned him to a service academy or created some form of post for training future officers. Stranger still, in February 1945, Eisenhower had ranked the top 36 officers "in order of merit based on the services rendered in the war." Bradley ranked number one; Patton came in fourth.

Months later, toward the end of Patton's tenure as governor, he and Eisenhower met one evening to discuss the future. Patton said, "There were only two jobs in the United States that I felt I could take . . . President of the Army War College . . . [or] Commanding General of the Army Ground Forces." The former position went to Gen. Leonard Gerow and the latter to Gen. Jake Devers. Both generals ranked lower than Patton on Eisenhower's list. Why were their needs prioritized over the needs of Patton—a man who, by Eisenhower's own estimation, served with greater merit than either of them?

At one point, Patton mused about retirement. Eisenhower asked him to delay such a move for three months, and Patton agreed. Later in life, Eisenhower would express guilt over Patton's fate but rationalized that there was no other billet to which he could be assigned. Marshall and Eisenhower, however, surely had the political leverage to do so at the time if they had wanted to. Perhaps it was impossible, perhaps they didn't want to grant favors to a man they now felt was nothing but a source of frustration, or perhaps it was something more nefarious. For whatever reason, when Patton returned to Europe in July, he was formally recognized as the military governor of Bavaria.

Excluding the cities of Bremen and Berlin, the U.S. occupation zone covered over 41,000 square miles. Of those 41,000 square miles, Patton was now governor of over half; 25,000 square miles and 9 million civilians, 2 million of whom were homeless. Of these 9 million civilians, roughly 75 percent were members of the Nazi Party in some capacity and were to be banned from most public positions. Repairing and rebuilding an entire region while simultaneously feeding, clothing, and caring for 9 million citizens, many of whom were brutal enemies only months earlier was daunting. Adding to it a policy that banned nearly three-quarters of the citizens from contributing meaningfully to the country made it almost impossible. Patton knew this well and detested the thought of taking on this command. But when Patton returned to Bavaria in July, he was greeted by a tremendous military parade, organized by his Third Army. The review included airplane escorts, the division band, and an honor guard. Patton was beaming. He shed the frustration of his visit home and resolved to embrace his new position in Germany with the same vigor he had brought to North Africa, Sicily, and France.

In Bavaria, Patton put on the mantle of watchdog. It is often said that great leaders need great challenges, just as "iron sharpens iron" (Proverbs 27:17).

There was no question that Patton was looking for his next great challenge. He didn't have to look far. Seeing firsthand the violence and atrocities committed by the Soviets in Berlin and countless sacked German villages and towns, Patton could already see the Red Menace growing. Meanwhile, the commanders and politicians were all adamant that equanimity and peace carry the day. America was war-weary, and the prospect of waging war with the Soviet Union was anathema to many Americans who simply wanted their boys to come home. Whether or not Patton recognized these realities is unclear. What is clear is that he was going to do all he could to stop it. Going above and beyond his duties as governor, he became the self-appointed protector of American interests and a public spokesman against the threat of Stalin and the menace of communism. As he noted in a letter to Beatrice, "We have destroyed what could have been a good race [the Germans] and we [are] about to replace them with Mongolian [i.e. Russian] savages. And all Europe will be communist."

But Patton's approach to governing the broken German people often ran counter to what his superiors deemed proper. His views on unconditional surrender began to shift, as he began to see it as a strategy that prolonged the ending of the war and gave

Stalin the upper hand. Patton, who had violently killed thousands of Huns on the battlefield, witnessed the maltreatment of German prisoners and the wholesale dismantling of the Nazi war machine. But the denazification policy offended him most. Under Allied military administration, the process proceeded rapidly throughout Germany. Nazi clergy were purged, street names were expunged, and war memorials were dismantled. Former Nazi Party members were excluded from business, banking, and industry as well as from the professions.

Patton had a population to feed, and heat, water, and electricity to supply. He had to begin reconstruction of basic infrastructure. Practically the only Germans who knew how to do these jobs had served during the Hitler regime as bureaucrats and administrators, and party membership was a job requirement at the time. Charles Province summarizes Patton's thinking on this issue well: "A lot of the people in Germany were Nazis simply because there was nothing else to do. It was the politics of the time; if you wanted to stay alive, you raised your arm and you said 'Heil Hitler,' and you said you were a Nazi." Indeed, as Patton opined to Eisenhower, "It is no more possible for a man to be a civil servant in Germany and not have paid lip service to Nazism than it is possible for a man to be a postmaster in America and not have paid at least lip service to the Democratic Party, or to the Republican Party when it is in power." This attitude would soon land him in more trouble.

Between a rock and a hard place, Patton was loath to fully implement the postwar policies prescribed by Supreme Headquarters Allied Expeditionary Force, or SHAEF. "Under our rules, which demand the total deNazification [sic] of Germany, we have to remove everyone who has ever expressed himself in any way as a Nazi or who has paid party dues," complained Patton. "It is very evident that anybody who was in business, irrespective of his real sentiments, had to say he was a Nazi and pay dues. The only young people who were not Nazis came out of the internment camps and are therefore either Jews or communists. We are certainly in a hard position as far as procuring civil servants is concerned."

Once the battle was over, Patton saw the Germans as just another defeated foe. Therefore, the mistreatment of postwar civilians, to his thinking, was a clash with the American tradition of due process. He would write, in letters home, that Americans fought the Revolution for our freedom and the Civil War to end slavery. What he was witnessing in postwar Europe—the apprehension of property and the removal from employment based on former Nazi loyalties—was a regression from those core principles. He would also speak out publicly on the vast number of POWs (upward of 20,000) abandoned by FDR and then Truman still under Russian occupation. As a result of his contrarian opinions, he was branded irrational and no longer trustworthy. George Marshall had Patton's phones tapped and requested he see a psychiatrist. By this point, Eisenhower was ready to join the chorus against Patton.

In his final months, Patton's perceptions of postwar Germany unraveled further as he concluded that the anti-German policies outlined at Yalta and given full U.S. support were not only extreme but also dangerous. He ignored his superiors and openly employed former Nazi military personnel to run the government in all facets. He also believed that these ex-soldiers were vital partners, essential in the near term for the defeat of the true enemy of the West, the Soviet Union. The press had a field day. For example, on September 19, 1945, Raymond Daniell reported in the *New York Times* that "Nazis still hold some of the best jobs in commerce and industry," referring to Patton's operation in Bavaria, thereby implying that the military was more concerned with preserving German industrial efficiency than fulfilling the objectives for which the war had been fought. But Patton's words, if allowed, exposed his real intentions: "I believe that

Germany should not be destroyed but rather should be rebuilt as a buffer against the real danger, which is Russia and its Bolshevism."

Patton called out the press as biased, and his piercing response was received as inflammatory and bordering on insubordination. In a letter to Beatrice he wrote, "All that sort of writing [about violations of fraternization and denazification policies] is done by Jews to get revenge." While it was certainly not uncommon for Americans at that time to be antisemitic, it was clear that Patton had no special love for the Jews, as he adopted them as the scapegoat for his woes as military governor. He angrily confided in his diary:

> There is a very apparent Semitic influence in the press. They are trying to do two things: First, implement Communism, and second, see that all business men [sic] of German ancestry and non-Jewish antecedents are thrown out of their jobs. They have utterly lost the Anglo-Saxon conception of justice and feel that a man can be kicked out because somebody else says he is a Nazi. They are evidently quite shocked when I told them I would kick nobody out without the successful proof of guilt before a court of law.

Rather than just sympathizing with the German people, however, Patton viewed the postwar struggle over who was fit to work in Germany in racialized terms; indeed, it seemed that, to Patton, the punishment of the German people had to be the fault of the Jews, whose own suffering during the war did not justify the policies of the occupation. In a mid-September diary entry, Patton made it clear that he believed the denazification policy to be a "virus . . . of a Semitic revenge against all Germans" and fumed about the supposed scheming of "the Jews who are lower than animals."

At face value, these statements are horrifically antisemitic and should be denounced as such. Patton reflected the racial attitudes of his time, and he had a history of hatred. For example, he loathed the population of North Africa: "The more I see of Arabs the less I think of them. By having studied them a good deal I have found out the trouble. They are the mixture of all the bad races on earth, and they get worse from west to east, because the eastern ones have had more crosses."

With Patton, there was no middle ground. If he was your friend, he was the most loyal friend you would ever have. If he was your enemy, there was no hell deep enough to satiate his condemnation. When he fought Germans, he made horrifying comments about the Germans. When he fought Italians, he made horrifying comments about Italians. When he planned to fight the Soviets, he made horrifying comments about the Soviets. Yet, in peace, he was often the first to extend the olive branch. There is a reality to war that is incompatible with peace. This is often why the more press exposure there is to a conflict, the quicker public opinion turns against it. Soldiers must hate their enemies, on some level, to fight them effectively. Patton understood this. The world did not.

While he was clearly a man with nineteenth-century views about race, Patton earnestly believed the denazification policy was wrongheaded, not least because, as a patriot, he recognized that the most significant threat to the free world was no longer the German people; rather, it was Stalin's Soviet Union that presented a serious danger to not only the West but also the world itself. He wrote to Beatrice: "I had never heard that we fought to de-natzify [sic] Germany—live and learn. What we are doing is to utterly destroy the only semi-modern state in Europe so that Russia can swallow the whole." Patton refused to permit such destruction on his watch. As such, he looked to rebuild Bavaria as quickly as possible, using just about anyone who was qualified for the positions that needed to be filled.

On September 22, when asked during a morning briefing at Bad Tölz about why he still had retained Nazis, Patton responded:

> I despise and abhor Nazis and Hitlerism as much as any-
> one. My record on that is clear and unchallengeable. It is to
> be found on battlefields from Morocco to Bad Tölz. . . .
> Now, more than half the Germans were Nazis and we
> would be in a hell of a fix if we removed all Nazi party
> members from office. The way I see it, this Nazi question is
> very much like a Democrat and Republican election fight.
> To get things done in Bavaria, after the complete disor-
> ganization and disruption of four years of war, we had to
> compromise with the devil a little. We had no alternative
> but to turn to the people who knew what to do and how
> to do it. So, for the time being we are compromising with
> the devil. . . . I don't like the Nazis any more than you do.
> I despise them. In the past three years I did my utmost to
> kill as many of them as possible. Now we are using them
> for lack of anyone better until we can get better people.

Patton's instincts would not only be justified by history but also can be seen even in our modern-day generals and political leaders. Exiling all those who were in power, even if well intentioned, will lead to disastrous consequences. Consider the case of the more recent Iraq War. Gen. Colin Powell acknowledged that the debath-ification of the Iraqi military would remove the only ruling infra-structure. Powell warned: "You need to understand, if you take out a government, take out a regime, guess who becomes the government and regime and is responsible for the country? You are. So if you break it, you own it." Though it would run counter to public opin-ion, debathification—like denazification before it—was the only policy that could have sustained those who had been defeated and keep out the encroaching enemy. More recently in Syria, the United States and Russia allowed President Bashar al-Assad to remain in place, forestalling a resurgence of the Muslim Brotherhood, which would have been an even more radical proposal. Powell concludes: "When you decide to get involved in a military operation in a place like Syria, you've got to be prepared, as we learned from Iraq and Afghanistan, to become the government, and I'm not sure any country, either the United States or I don't hear of anyone else, who's willing to take on that responsibility."

Patton also spoke forcefully about the Allied prisoners of war, or POWs, perhaps numbering as many as 20,000, whom he believed had been abandoned first by Roosevelt and then by Truman. By superficially denoting captured Germans not as POWs but as "disarmed enemy forces," American forces were only permitted to feed them "starvation rations"—just enough food so that mass deaths would not occur.

During a press conference on September 22, reporters pressured Patton regarding denazification efforts in Bavaria.

Subsequent accounts by the *New York Times* and other outlets characterized Patton as respecting Germans more than Soviets, former enemies. Patton was clearly out of touch with the American public's ideas about why the war had been fought to begin with, and his remarks resulted in a barrage of criticism against the Army.

As such, Patton had once more put himself and his superiors in a rough position even as the American public was becoming aware of the Holocaust.

Taking the Gag Off

Little did Patton know that he was sowing the seeds of his own demise by being so forthright. A week after Patton made the initial inflammatory statement, Eisenhower called him to his headquarters, where the Supreme Allied Commander confronted his stubborn subordinate. Struggling with his task, Eisenhower, ever the politician, told Patton, "Your greatest virtue is also your greatest fault. It's your audacity." Far from an insult; Patton embodied the gospel of Napoleon: *l'audace, l'audace, toujours l'audace!* (or audacity, audacity, always audacity!). But this ran directly counter to Patton's own thinking, which was that his most double-edged trait was his "honesty and lack of ulterior motive." In short, Patton had insulted the Russians and, in so doing, had made Eisenhower look bad. Only a few days later, Eisenhower stripped Patton of command of his beloved Third Army, which Patton had once lauded as "the Eighth Wonder of the World." Instead, Patton would now command the Fifteenth Army, tasked with collecting, archiving, and writing a history of the war.

Though ostensibly a change of command, the October 2 issue of *Stars and Stripes* announcing the decision carried the headline "PATTON FIRED." It was an odd twist of fate that the general, who prided himself on being a student of history, was now commanding a unit tasked with collecting, archiving, and writing a history of the war. The normally critical *New York Times* was surprisingly sympathetic:

> Patton has passed from current controversy into history.
> There he will have an honored place. . . . He was obviously
> in a post [for] which he was unsuited by temperament,
> training or experience to fill. It was a mistake to suppose a
> free-swinging fighter could acquire overnight the capacities
> of a wise administrator. His removal by General Eisenhower
> was an acknowledgment of that mistake. . . . For all his
> showmanship he was a scientific soldier, a thorough military
> student. . . . He reaped no laurels from the peace, but those
> he won in war will remain green for a long time.

Despite Patton's interest in studying the war because of the "lessons learned" literature he could write for the Army, it was a shabby payoff. He hobbled a little but remained on his feet and even managed to produce a little smile on his pale, thin lips—probably by forgetting the humiliation of these days and thinking of the not-too-distant future. He could not see any yield in being a martyr too soon. Following the encounter with Eisenhower, Patton wrote: "I will resign when I have finished this job. I hate to do it but I have been gagged all my life, and whether they are appreciated or not, America needs some honest men who dare to say what they think, not what they think people want them to think."

Patton would eventually confess:

It is my belief that when the catchword "denazification" has worn itself out and when people see it is merely a form of stimulating Russian Bolshevism, there will be a flop of the pendulum in the opposite direction. In a sense, I'm glad to get out, as I hate the role we are forced to play and the unethical means we are required to use.

In hindsight, his actions take on a different perspective. Almost every controversial decision of his administration would be commonly adopted within only years of his dismissal. The denazification program was abandoned in the early 1950s and is reviled today in both America and Germany. The West eventually recognized the threat of the Soviet Union, though by the time it did it was almost too late, as it scrambled to form the North Atlantic Treaty Organization, or NATO, in 1949. The German army was reorganized and rearmed. Field Marshal Erich von Manstein, a man found guilty on nine counts of war crimes during the Nuremberg trials, was released from prison after only four years and appointed to reestablish the German military. Last, and most important, halting the spread of communism became the crux of American foreign policy until the fall of the Soviet Union. It seems Patton's greatest accomplishment was how far ahead of his time he ended up being. Sadly, as with all prophets, this perspective could only be attained in the years following his actions. He found no such comfort in 1945.

It seemed his only chance to speak freely was outside the military, as he regretfully observed, "I think that I'd like to resign from the Army so that I could go home and say what I have to say." But some did not want this to happen. Indeed, as previously mentioned, on May 10, Eisenhower had lectured his fellow officers "on the necessity for solidarity in the event that any of us are called before a Congressional Committee." If Patton were to go home and tell the American people about what he considered to be serious mistakes made during the war, it would spell trouble for Eisenhower, Bradley, and others.

He once again needed to be gagged, lest he reveal the secret errors of the war and expose the fallout narrative of how, at key times, those superiors and statesmen chose politics over the dirty business of war. Patton was challenging the forces (and limitations) of power, and it would make sense that those powers would want his challenging voice removed, but how far would his destiny play out in the final days. How would he preserve his legacy not only as one of the greatest American generals.

....

CHAPTER EIGHT

The True Cover-up

Like his heroes of antiquity and the Middle Ages, Patton would exit the world stage an admired but deeply flawed character. He has been parodied in books and movies as a warmonger, an exuberant anticommunist, and a heartless commander. Conspiracy theories promptly surfaced following Patton's untimely accident on the back roads of Heidelberg. Many believed (and believe still) that Patton had crossed the line with his wartime adversaries in the political and military class. The nature and timing of his death, therefore, were suspect, a cover-up.

Yet, in the unpacking of the incident that would ultimately take his life, we uncover the true heart of Patton. At his core, Patton was a man of honor.

A Man for the Ages

After the dust had settled from his latest public snafu, Patton needed a break. He felt as if he had been screaming his warnings about the Soviets into the void, and the void would not respond. December 9, 1945, was supposed to be a day of relaxation for Patton, as he and some of his staff were to go pheasant hunting. It was to be Patton's last day in Germany before he flew to England and then sailed back to the United States. Patton's close friend and chief of staff, Hobart "Hap" Gay, noticing that his boss had been depressed due to recent developments, had suggested the trip on the night of December 8, in hopes of cheering Patton up. They set out the next morning, which was frigid and cloudless.

It is rather telling that for all the heroes of antiquity and the Middle Ages Patton was so fond of, there was a clear omission. His father had read *The Iliad* and *The Odyssey* to him from a young age, and he could quote Hector of Troy, Breaker of Horses, and his great nemesis Achilles with ease. He had visited Hannibal's great battlefields and the ruins of his once-proud city, Carthage. He had celebrated the genius of Alexander the Great, the courage of Leonidas, and the brilliance of Julius Caesar. But these heroes all had one thing in common: They were all killed with honor. As Patton had said, he wanted to be killed by "the last bullet of the last battle of the last war."

His heroes were all men who fought to the bitter end. Those few who lived, died in exile. Hector died in single combat with Achilles, who was, in turn, killed in battle. Despite numerous victories, Hannibal was defeated, his country was immolated, and he was later killed in exile. Leonidas was killed, decapitated, and crucified; Alexander the Great died at age 32; and Caesar was betrayed and stabbed to death. Few, if any, of his heroes lived "happily ever after." Yet, for all his reading of antiquity, it is telling that Patton rarely invoked Cincinnatus.

Lucius Quinctius Cincinnatus was the great general of Rome who, when his country was desperate, assumed complete power, defeated the Aequi, and then relinquished his command and control to live the life of a quiet farmer. He was the model for the life of George Washington. In the pantheon of Patton's heroes, Cincinnatus is omitted. His absence, the absence of leaders who lived similar lives, and Patton's many apocalyptic quotes in life make one thing clear: He expected to die in combat. He saw his destiny as a glorious death in battle.

Patton had faced a great destiny and achieved his glory, but he lived. What was he to do now? He was not one to lay down his sword and return to the farm, as Washington had done. Would a greater destiny be achieved in a desperate battle with the Soviet Union? Or worse, was destiny finished with the veteran general? The depression he suffered leading up to that gray day in December 9 starts to make sense when one realizes that, for the first time since the interwar years, Patton was questioning his place in history.

Patton and his retinue had traveled for several hours when they passed through Mannheim. After an unplanned stop at nearby Roman ruins, Patton's newly assigned driver, Horace Woodring, who had been partying the night before, brought the Cadillac to a halt at a railroad crossing, waiting for a train to pass.

After it passed, Woodring accelerated again. In the opposite lane, a truck driven by Technician Fifth Rank (T/5) Robert L. Thompson suddenly turned left without using a turn signal. Woodring and Gay, both riding with Patton, had been temporarily distracted when Patton pointed out some abandoned vehicles on the side of the road. When Woodring's gaze returned to its rightful place, he saw Thompson's 2.5-ton truck careening toward the Cadillac. He steered to the left, hoping to avoid a collision, but the truck T-boned Patton's vehicle.

While Gay, Woodring, and Thompson escaped without serious injury, Patton was not so lucky. The general was half-scalped by the overhead light in the car, his nose was broken, and he was paralyzed from the neck down. Patton recognized that he had been paralyzed and, after asking if Woodring and Gay were all right, told them, "Work my fingers for me. Take and rub my arms and shoulders and rub them hard." At the end of his leave in the United States during the summer, he had confided to his daughters that he felt he would not see them again. He died in a Heidelberg hospital 12 days after the accident.

But was it really an accident? In the wake of Patton's death, many hypothesized that the general's demise was not simply a freakish tragedy but rather part of a conspiracy to eliminate him once and for all. While some pinned the "accident" on Soviet operatives, others believed that the masterminds behind the alleged plot were actually those higher-ups in the American military and political chain of command who were most threatened by Patton and his willingness to voice unpopular opinions. After all, his desire to inform the American people of the strategic errors made during the war constituted a serious danger to his superiors. Similarly, Patton's warnings were an irritant to Stalin, who did not want Patton to spoil his plans to "win the peace" as he lowered the Iron Curtain over Central and Eastern Europe. If Patton had one ally in opinion, it was Winston Churchill, who even secretly planned a potential offensive against the Soviets, should their premonitions prove real.

But in the end, while his hate for the Russians or his contentions with Eisenhower and some in his own leadership could provide motivation for a potential "silencing," none of the basic facts or logistics can be corroborated. There is simply no plausible evidence to substantiate the conspiracy theories. Carlo D'Este, author of *Patton: Genius of War*, concludes:

> Those who suggest that Patton was somehow murdered
> have failed to provide the slightest evidence of how anyone
> could have planned such a caper or ensured that Patton's
> Cadillac would be momentarily stopped for the passage
> of a train at the crossing just down the street from the
> scene of the accident. Other than a handful of men on his
> personal staff, no one even knew where Patton would be,

what route he would follow, or what time he would arrive at his destination.

The Tragedy of Patton

Patton, like most of his heroes, was certainly no diplomat. He was blunt and opinionated. Some would argue he was a world-class narcissist. So his threat to "take off the gag" had some running scared. Patton warned against Stalin's betrayal of the West, even as the ink dried on the settlements at Yalta. Yet, within three years, Patton's words echoed in the chill of the Cold War as the Soviet Union blocked all Western transportation corridors into Berlin in an attempt to seize control of the city that Patton had once sought to secure. The Berlin Airlift of 1948–1949 gave credence to Patton's cautions. Moreover, what had been characterized as insubordination by Patton in the fall of 1945 proved to be sound policy by 1948, as U.S. officials revived the careers of some Nuremberg criminals to help rebuild the German army in defense of West Berlin against Soviet aggression. So, within four years of the war's end, with the Berlin Airlift and the creation of NATO, Patton's recommendations had become official American foreign and military policy. As historian Victor Davis Hanson puts it, "the problem was, he [Patton] was four or five years too early in [voicing] his assessment."

If Patton's discernment on and off the battlefield was accurate, if his strategies proved correct time and time again, then why were Western leaders compelled to grind down the wheels of his tanks?

In December 1945, in a hospital bed in Heidelberg, Patton would "smile back" at death. Though his death is tainted with suspicion, how could a four-star general suffer a car accident with an Army truck, and yet there was no investigation, no court-martial for those involved? The military, known for its thoroughness, did not take any action. After all, a wounded general in a car accident could invite a Russian assassin, as would that general's vulnerability if left in a hospital—particularly one that was covered by a media circus, in which many journalists dressed as orderlies to stand at Patton's side, perhaps to watch him sip his final glasses of whiskey.

Aside from the lack of an accident report, lack of an autopsy, and the suspicions of many of his own soldiers, the key to understanding why so many theories have existed is clearly in the fact that the handling of Patton's death *seems* like a cover-up. Why was the driver who crashed the Army truck into Patton's vehicle able to walk away without penalty? We know that Thompson had been drunk and on a joyride with his buddies, and we know that as the MPs arrived at the accident, Patton, even though paralyzed from the neck down, had been cognizant enough to make it clear that it had been an accident. He had ordered the MPs not to charge Thompson or his companions and to keep the accident off their record. Even though his men's carelessness had resulted in the accident that ultimately killed him, Patton, according to Charles Province, did not want them to suffer as a result "because they were his men in his army, and he was still, after all this time, looking after them." Perhaps he was recalling Robert E. Lee's words when he told his soldiers, "Go home all you boys who fought with me and help build up the shattered fortunes of our old state."

All in all, it is quite clear that asserting that Patton's death was the culmination of an elaborate assassination conspiracy is grasping at straws, at best. While true that some aspects of his death are unclear or even mysterious, and although some of the facts can be explained by the motivations of his public opponents, as conspiracy theories, the alignment of such theories with some of the facts is hardly enough to prove them. Of course, such conspiracy theories cannot simply be dismissed outright without examining the facts, not least because the theories are often used as means of explaining a seemingly inexplicable tragedy, thereby giving closure to those who experienced it.

/ Covering Tracks

But if the circumstances of Patton's death were not the cover-up, then what was? For Patton's superiors, it was surely the fact that the strategic mistakes of the war would go unannounced for some time, thereby preventing the destruction of the political and military careers of Eisenhower, Bradley, and others. To quote Province again, "they [Patton's superiors] didn't kill him, but by God, they were glad he was gone." The true cover-up was Patton's actions to protect his men from court-martial, driven by his sense of honor. Indeed, there is no small irony in the fact that by looking after his men, Patton inadvertently made an already-odd scenario even more mysterious, thereby providing conspiracy theorists with a great starting point (the lack of an official investigation, etc.).

Conspiracy or not, Patton's death proved to be a tragedy for the American people and the world, a fact which the American public recognized surprisingly quickly, given how controversial the general had been. Martin Blumenson posits that because Patton did not die immediately but struggled valiantly in his final battle, he gave the press

> a chance to recall at length his triumphs and [feature] his successes. His swashbuckling and color, his flamboyance and profanity were no longer deemed extraneous to his accomplishments. They were all part of his image, and his image in large part was responsible for his victories. As an enthralled public followed his last struggle in the hospital with sympathy, they came to appreciate his impact on the war, to be grateful for his results, to admire what he had

done. . . . The understanding and applause, together with the profound grief at his death, transformed him almost at once into a folk hero, a man who was already a legend.

In death, Patton effectively accomplished what he had chased his whole life—the status of a military legend. In the meantime, however, both his superiors (especially Eisenhower and Bradley) and his enemies (Stalin and his cronies) likely breathed a collective sigh of relief, knowing that the man most able to ruin their plans no longer had the breath to do so.

Patton, as his only equal Gen. MacArthur would later say, had not died but faded away. But will the history of the Cold War be the ultimate arbiter of not only his death but also his legacy?

Epilogue

When he died, Patton had recently turned 60. He had seen and known war, and though his end did not come on the battlefield, he had fought valiantly to lead what, by some accounts, was the greatest army that ever existed. He performed like a warrior of old, who had driven his tanks not only across France but also, in his mind and the minds of his men, on the road to valor. He was willing to sacrifice himself as an example of a leader, and he cared little about power or politics. He was loved and hated, but no one could doubt the respect he deserved.

Patton's *élan vital* was essential on the battlefield, necessary to face the fiercest of enemies in the Nazis, whose generals considered Patton their only equal. They understood he had prepared his life for this moment and stated at the start of the war that all the moments of his life had led to that one moment in time. But the choice to call upon him after the horrific loss at Kasserine Pass was made with reluctance, and that reluctance would carry throughout the war. The same reluctance, as Victor Davis Hanson explains, comes from the tradition of the antihero familiar to the American Western. Though conventional heroes like Eisenhower and Bradley were more beloved and had more polish as diplomats, they did not defeat the Germans in Africa, lead the Sicilian invasion, break out on the Normandy beaches, roll back the Germans through France, or swoop north in a blizzard to cut off Hitler's Battle of the Bulge.

Patton was cut from an earlier age of which he believed he was the American manifestation of the great generals. To his thinking, it was his job to steel his men (indeed the world) against a brutal enemy. War was a purge, a galvanizing of the will that would remove the dross of cowardice and weakness, much of the same fears he battled in his own protected childhood. As war has always been, it was the rite of passage, the means whereby boys always become men. America was the final phase of that fighting spirit of the West, dating back to Cincinnatus, Alexander, Washington, and now these GIs.

His challenges to Allied strategies during and after the war may have lacked tact, but were they wrong? He was head and shoulders above his peers on the battlefield. He was right about Stalin, with his warning against Russia's betrayal of the West finally proven correct with the Soviet blockade of Berlin in 1948, a move that would necessitate the legendary Berlin Airlift. The Soviet Union's threats, birthed by Stalin, would persist for decades.

In light of the events that have unfolded in the more than 75 years since World War II concluded, Patton still warns us from the grave: "You mark my words. Don't ever forget them. Someday we will have to fight them and it will take six years and cost us six million lives." Patton was a prophetic character who foresaw the future confrontation that would consume the West and the Soviet Union for much of the second half of the twentieth century. He believed in the righteous cause of the military and revealed his plans to fight those who aimed to destroy its morale and who endangered America's future by not opposing the growing Soviet threat. He was willing and able to confront these foes, whom he viewed, in the words of Victor Davis Hanson, as "agents of evil and a danger to a democratic society." But he was made to stand down.

Always the student of military history, he would clearly understand and therefore warn, "If we have to fight them, now is the time; from now on, we will get weaker and they will get stronger."

Shortly after Patton's demise, the countries of Eastern Europe were crushed by Soviet tyranny. For decades, the United States fought proxy wars against communist aggression in Korea, Cuba, Vietnam, Iraq, and Afghanistan. Millions of innocents were tortured, raped, and murdered under the red flag.

As Patton's memorial and burial services were planned, his belongings were packed up for the final time: official papers, stag horns, footlockers, a big wardrobe, two steamer trunks, several canes, a sword, books, a portable typewriter, his portrait (a Christmas present for Beatrice), helmets, dictaphones, scrapbooks, and suitcases. After the memorial service, Patton's body was ceremoniously transported, by train, to the Luxembourg American Cemetery and Memorial in Hamm, Luxembourg. There he was laid to rest under a plain white cross bearing his name, rank, and serial number alongside the fallen men of the Third Army.

Patton's diaries are littered with criticisms of Eisenhower and Bradley, and at times he found fault with how the war had been executed and how he believed politics and blindness toward Stalin's intentions came at the expense of American GIs and world peace. It seems that one of the greatest lessons to be learned from Patton is that while some generals, like Eisenhower, were great because they understood the importance of diplomacy, others, like Patton, were great because they knew what was needed to win the war. Patton understood the soul of war and the spiritual means by which to lead men into battle. He also knew the bloody price men pay for others to live in peace. In serving the "land of the free and the home of the brave," he would not—indeed, could not—be gagged.

....

Patton's Bookshelf

George Patton was an accomplished student of military history. Despite a lifelong learning disability, most likely a combination of what today would be diagnosed as dyslexia and ADD, Patton was one of the most well-read military leaders in modern history. Through sheer will and discipline, he developed a voracious appetite for books, particularly biographies and memoirs of the world's great leaders—from Hannibal and Caesar to Napoleon and Robert E. Lee. Patton's principal biographer, Martin Blumenson, wrote, "These commanders who exhibited self-confidence, enthusiasm, and bravery became [Patton's] models, and he absorbed their genius."

Patton's reading interests were deep and wide. For example, in addition to great military geniuses—von Treitschke, von Clausewitz, von Schlieffen, von Seeckt, and others of that genre—he had an affinity for great poetry and literature, including Shakespeare, Sir Walter Scott, and Arthur Conan Doyle.

Following is a short list of books that shaped and informed Patton, both as a young boy and as a West Point cadet and throughout his storied career as America's greatest combat general of World War II.

The Bible

Homer's *The Iliad* and *The Odyssey*

The works of William Shakespeare

The complete works of Rudyard Kipling

Commentaries by Julius Caesar

Genghis Khan, Alexander of Macedon, and other biographies by Harold Lamb

Maxims of Napoleon and all the authoritative military biographies of Napoleon

R. E. Lee: A Biography by Douglas Southall Freeman

Memoirs of Erich Ludendorff, Paul von Hindenburg, and Marshall Foch

Memoirs of Ulysses S. Grant and George McClellan

Stonewall Jackson by G. F. R. Henderson

The Crowd: A Study of the Popular Mind by Gustave Le Bon

Alexander the Great by Arthur Weigall

Generalship: Its Diseases and Their Cures by J. F. C. Fuller

Lee's Lieutenants: A Study in Command by Douglas Southall Freeman

The Art of War in the Middle Ages by Charles Oman

Fifteen Decisive Battles of the World by Sir Edward S. Creasy

History of the Peloponnesian War by Thucydides

The Influence of Sea Power trilogy by Alfred Thayer Mahan

The Decline and Fall of the Roman Empire by Edward Gibbon

Gallipoli Diary by Sir Ian Hamilton

The Prince by Niccolo Machiavelli

The Years of Victory and the Years of Endurance by Arthur Bryant

The works of Sir Winston S. Churchill

....

Timeline

A chronology of key events in the life and career of General George S. Patton (1885–1945), army officer and author.

1885, November 11

Born, San Gabriel, California

1903–1904

Attended Virginia Military Institute, Lexington, Virginia

1909

Graduated, United States Military Academy, West Point, New York

Assigned to Fifteenth United States Cavalry, Fort Sheridan, Illinois, and Fort Myer, Virginia

1910

Married Beatrice Banning Ayer

1912

> Member, American team, XII Olympiad, Stockholm, Sweden, finishing fifth in modern pentathlon

1912–1913

> Attended French cavalry school, Saumur, France

1913

> Graduated, United States Cavalry School, Fort Riley, Kansas

1913–1915

> Instructor in weapons, United States Cavalry School, Fort Riley, Kansas

1915–1916

> Assigned to Eighth United States Cavalry, Fort Bliss, Texas

1916–1917

> Aide-de-camp to General John J. Pershing, Mexican Punitive Expedition

1917

> Aide-de-camp to General John J. Pershing, Commander-in-Chief, American Expeditionary Forces
>
> Commanded Headquarters Troop, American Expeditionary Forces

1917–1918

> Detailed as first member of American Tank Corps and attended French Tank School, Camplieu, France
>
> Organized American Tank School, Langres, France

1918

Promoted to temporary rank of lieutenant colonel

1918–1921

Commander, 304th Tank Brigade

1919–1921

Invented a coaxial gun mount

1921–1922

Commander, First Squadron, Third United States Cavalry, Fort Myer, Virginia

1923–1928

United States Army General Staff, Boston, Massachusetts, 1923–1924; Hawaii, 1924–1928

1928–1931

Served in Office of the Chief of Cavalry, United States Army

1932

Graduated, United States Army War College

1932–1935

Executive Officer, Third United States Cavalry, Fort Myer, Virginia

1934

Promoted to lieutenant colonel

1935–1937

G-2, United States Army General Staff, Hawaiian Department

1938

Promoted to colonel

Commander, Fifth United States Cavalry, Fort Clark, Texas

1938–1940

Commander, Third United States Cavalry, Fort Myer, Virginia

1940

Promoted to brigadier general

1940–1941

Commander, Second Armored Brigade, Second Armored Division, Fort Benning, Georgia

1941

Promoted to major general

1941–1942

Commander, Second Armored Division, Fort Benning, Georgia

1942

Commander, I Armored Corps, First and Second Armored Divisions

1942–1943

> Commanded Western Task Force during Allied landings and subsequent campaign in North Africa
>
> Transferred to command of United States II Corps

1943

> Promoted to lieutenant general
>
> Relinquished command of II Corps to Omar Nelson Bradley
>
> Resumed command of I Armored Corps in preparation for invasion of Sicily

1943–1944

> Commanded Seventh United States Army in Sicilian campaign

1944

> Ordered to England to take command of Third United States Army in preparation for invasion of France

1944–1945

> Commanded Third United States Army in drive across France, Germany, Czechoslovakia, and Austria

1945

> Commander, Fifteenth United States Army

1945, December 21

> Died

Bibliography

PRIMARY SOURCES

Blumenson, Martin, ed. *The Patton Papers, 1940–1945*. Boston, MA: Houghton Mifflin Company, 1974.

Province, Charles M., ed. *Military Essays and Articles by George S. Patton*. San Diego, CA: George S. Patton Jr. Historical Society, 2012.

George S. Patton Papers, Manuscript Division, Library of Congress, https://www.loc.gov/collect ions/george-s-patton-diaries/about-this-collection/.

Patton Jr., George S., and Paul D. Harkins. *War as I Knew It*. Boston: Houghton Mifflin Company, 1947.

Peters, Gerhard, and John T. Woolley. The American Presidency Project. http://www.presidency.ucsb.edu/ws/?pid=16408.

SECONDARY SOURCES

Allison, Graham. *Destined for War*. New York: Houghton-Mifflin Harcourt, 2017.

Axelrod, Alan. *Patton: A Biography*. New York: St. Martin's Griffin, 2009.

———. *Patton's Drive: The Making of America's Greatest General.* Guilford, CT: Lyons Press, 2009.

Beevor, Antony. *The Fall of Berlin, 1945.* New York: Viking Press, 2002.

Bergen, Doris L, *War and Genocide: A Concise History of the Holocaust,* 3rd ed. (Lanham, MD: Rowman & Littlefield, 2016).

Berthon, Simon, and Joanna Potts. *Warlords: An Extraordinary Re-Creation of World War II Through the Eyes and Minds of Hitler, Roosevelt, Churchill, and Stalin.* Cambridge, MA: Da Capo Press, 2007.

Blumenson, Martin. *Patton: The Man Behind the Legend, 1885–1945.* New York: William Morrow and Company, 1985.

———. *The Battle of the Generals: The Untold Story of the Falaise Pocket—The Campaign That Should Have Won World War II.* New York: William Morrow, 1993.

Churchill's Darkest Decision, National Geographic Channel, https://www.youtube.com/watch?v=Nyku1lSRiFU.

"Concerning the International Situation," *Works,* Vol. 6, January–November, 1924.

Delaforce, Patrick. *Smashing the Atlantic Wall: The Destruction of Hitler's Coastal Fortresses.* Barnsley, UK: Pen & Sword Military, 2006.

D'Este, Carlo, *Eisenhower: A Soldier's Life* (New York: Holt, 2003).

D'Este, Carlo. *Patton: A Genius for War.* New York: HarperCollins, 1995.

de Zayas, Alfred-Maurice. *A Terrible Revenge: The Ethnic Cleansing of the East European Germans*, 2nd ed. New York: Palgrave MacMillan, 2006.

Dobbs, Michael. *Six Months in 1945: FDR, Stalin, Churchill, and Truman—from World War to Cold War*. New York: Vintage Books, 2012.

Eisenhower, John S. D., with Joanne Thompson Eisenhower. *Yanks: The Epic Story of the American Army in World War I*. New York: The Free Press, 2001.

Farago, Ladislas. *The Last Days of Patton*. Yardley, PA: Westholme Publishers, 2011.

Forty, George. *Patton's Third Army at War*. Philadelphia: Casemate Publishers, 2015.

Gilbert, Martin. *Churchill: A Life*. New York: Henry Holt and Company, 1991.

Grumet, Gerald W. "General George S. Patton, Jr. and the Conquest of Fear." *Psychological Reports* (August 2009).

Hanson, Victor Davis. *The Soul of Battle: From Ancient Times to the Present Day, How Three Liberators Vanquished Tyranny*. New York: Free Press, 1999.

Hastings, Max. *OVERLORD: D-Day and the Battle for Normandy*. New York: Simon & Schuster, 1984.

Havardi, Jeremy. *The Greatest Briton: Essays on Winston Churchill's Life and Political Philosophy*. London: Shepheard-Walwyn Publishers, 2009.

Hirshon, Stanley P. *General Patton: A Soldier's Life*. New York: HarperCollins Publishers, 2002.

Irving, David. *The War Between the Generals: Inside the High Command*. New York: Congdon & Lattès, 1981.

Jordan, Jonathan W. *Brothers, Rivals, Victors: Eisenhower, Patton, Bradley, and the Partnership That Drove the Allied Conquest in Europe*. New York: NAL/Caliber, 2011.

Keane, Michael. *Patton: Blood, Guts, and Prayer*. Washington, DC: Regnery History, 2012.

Kengor, Paul. *Dupes: How America's Adversaries Have Manipulated Progressives for a Century*. Wilmington, DE: Intercollegiate Studies Institute, 2010.

Kissinger, Henry. *Diplomacy*. New York: Simon & Schuster, 1994.

Large, David Clay. *Berlin*. New York: Basic Books, 2001.

Lengel, Edward G. *To Conquer Hell: The Meuse-Argonne, 1918— The Epic Battle That Ended the First World War*. New York: Henry Holt and Company, 2008.

Mahoney, William J. *Diseases, Disorders, and Diagnoses of Historical Individuals*. Atlanta, GA: Anaphora Literary Press, 2015.

Nye, Roger H. *The Patton Mind: The Professional Development of an Extraordinary Leader*. Garden City Park, NY: Avery Publishing Group, 1993.

O'Reilly, Bill, and Martin Dugard. *Killing Patton: The Strange Death of World War II's Most Audacious General*. New York: Henry Holt and Company, 2014.

Pipes, Richard. *Communism: A History*. New York: The Modern Library, 2003.

Province, Charles M., ed. *Military Essays and Articles by George S. Patton*. San Diego, CA: George S. Patton Jr. Historical Society, 2012.

———. *The Unknown Patton*. New York: Hippocrene Books, 1983.

Rees, Laurence. *World War II Behind Closed Doors: Stalin, the Nazis and the West*. New York: Pantheon Books, 2008.

Robert Cowley, ed. *The Cold War: A Military History*. New York: Random House, 2005.

Showalter, Dennis. *Patton and Rommel: Men of War in the Twentieth Century*. New York: Berkley Caliber, 2005.

Smith, Gaddis. *American Diplomacy during the Second World War, 1941–1945*. New York: John Wiley and Sons, 1965.

Smith, Jean Edward, *Eisenhower in War and Peace* (New York: Random House, 2013).

Sweeney, Michael S. *Secrets of Victory: The Office of Censorship and the American Press and Radio in World War II*. Chapel Hill, NC: University of North Carolina Press, 2001.

von Rauch, Georg. *A History of Soviet Russia*, 6th ed. Translated by Peter Jacobsohn and Annette Jacobsohn. New York: Praeger, 1972.

Waddington, Loran, *Hitler's Crusade: Bolshevism and the Myth of the International Jewish Conspiracy* (London: Taurus Academic Studies, 2007).

Weingartner, James J. "Massacre at Biscari: Patton and an American War Crime." *The Historian* 52, no. 1 (November 1989): 243–249.

Wilcox, Robert K. *Target: Patton—The Plot to Assassinate General George S. Patton*. Washington, DC: Regnery Publishing, 2008.

Patton's Speech to
the Third Army

(Delivered in various forms—without notes—to motivate the troops between February, 1944 and June 5, 1944—the day before D-Day.)

No bastard ever won a war by dying for his country. He won it by making the other poor dumb bastard die for his country.

Be seated.

Men, all this stuff you hear about America not wanting to fight, wanting to stay out of the war, is a lot of horse dung. Americans love to fight. All real Americans love the sting and clash of battle. When you were kids, you all admired the champion marble shooter, the fastest runner, the big-league ball players and the toughest boxers. Americans love a winner and will not tolerate a loser. Americans play to win all the time. That's why Americans have never lost and will never lose a war. The very thought of losing is hateful to Americans. Battle is the most significant competition in which a man can indulge. It brings out all that is best and it removes all that is base.

You are not all going to die. Only two percent of you right here today would be killed in a major battle. Every man is scared in his first action. If he says he's not, he's a goddamn liar. But the real hero is the man who fights even though he's scared. Some men will get over their fright in a minute under fire, some take an hour, and for some it takes days. But the real man never lets his fear of death overpower his honor, his sense of duty to his country, and his innate manhood.

All through your army career you men have bitched about what you call 'this chicken-shit drilling.' That is all for a purpose—to ensure instant obedience to orders and to create constant alertness. This must be bred into every soldier. I don't give a fuck for a man who is not always on his toes. But the drilling has made veterans of all you men. You are ready! A man has to be alert all the time if he expects to keep on breathing. If not, some German son-of-a-bitch will sneak up behind him and beat him to death with a sock full of shit. There are four hundred neatly marked graves in Sicily, all because one man went to sleep on the job—but they are German graves, because we caught the bastard asleep before his officer did.

An army is a team. It lives, eats, sleeps, and fights as a team. This individual hero stuff is bullshit. The bilious bastards who write that stuff for the *Saturday Evening Post* don't know any more about real battle than they do about fucking. And we have the best team—we have the finest food and equipment, the best spirit and the best men in the world. Why, by God, I actually pity these poor bastards we're going up against.

All the real heroes are not storybook combat fighters. Every single man in the army plays a vital role. So don't ever let up. Don't ever think that your job is unimportant. What if every truck driver decided that he didn't like the whine of the shells and turned yellow and jumped headlong into a ditch? That cowardly bastard could say to himself, 'Hell, they won't miss me, just one man in thousands.' What if every man said that? Where in the hell would we be then? No, thank God, Americans don't say that. Every man does his job. Every man is important. The ordnance men are needed to supply the guns, the quartermaster is needed to bring up the food and clothes for us because where we are going there isn't a hell of a lot to steal. Every last damn man in the mess hall, even the one who boils the water to keep us from getting the GI shits, has a job to do.

Each man must think not only of himself, but think of his buddy fighting alongside him. We don't want yellow cowards in the army. They should be killed off like flies. If not, they will go back home after the war, goddamn cowards, and breed more cowards. The brave men will breed more brave men. Kill off the goddamn cowards and we'll have a nation of brave men.

One of the bravest men I saw in the African campaign was on a telegraph pole in the midst of furious fire while we were moving toward Tunis. I stopped and asked him what the hell he was doing up there. He answered, 'Fixing the wire, sir.' 'Isn't it a little unhealthy up there right now?' I asked. 'Yes sir, but this goddamn wire has got to be fixed.' I asked, 'Don't those planes strafing the road bother you?' And he answered, 'No sir, but you sure as hell do.' Now, there was a real soldier. A real man. A man who devoted all he had to his duty, no matter how great the odds, no matter how seemingly insignificant his duty appeared at the time.

And you should have seen the trucks on the road to Gabès. Those drivers were magnificent. All day and all night they crawled along those son-of-a-bitch roads, never stopping, never deviating from their course with shells bursting all around them. Many of the men drove over 40 consecutive hours. We got through on good old American guts. These were not combat men. But they were soldiers with a job to do. They were part of a team. Without them the fight would have been lost.

Sure, we all want to go home. We want to get this war over with. But you can't win a war lying down. The quickest way to get it over with is to get the bastards who started it. We want to get the hell over there and clean the goddamn thing up, and then get at those purple-pissing Japs. The quicker they are whipped, the quicker we go home. The shortest way home is through Berlin and Tokyo. So keep moving. And when we get to Berlin, I am personally going to shoot that paper-hanging son-of-a-bitch Hitler.

When a man is lying in a shell hole, if he just stays there all day, a Boche will get him eventually. The hell with that. My men don't dig foxholes. Foxholes only slow up an offensive. Keep moving. We'll win this war, but we'll win it only by fighting and showing the Germans that we've got more guts than they have or ever will have. We're not just going to shoot the bastards, we're going to rip out their living goddamned guts and use them to grease the treads of our tanks. We're going to murder those lousy Hun cocksuckers by the bushel-fucking-basket.

Some of you men are wondering whether or not you'll chicken out under fire. Don't worry about it. I can assure you that you'll all do your duty. War is a bloody business, a killing business. The Nazis are the enemy. Wade into them, spill their blood or they will spill yours. Shoot them in the guts. Rip open their belly. When shells are hitting all around you and you wipe the dirt from your face and you realize that it's not dirt, it's the blood and gut of what was once your best friend, you'll know what to do.

I don't want any messages saying 'I'm holding my position.' We're not holding a goddamned thing. We're advancing constantly and we're not interested in holding anything except the enemy's balls. We're going to hold him by his balls and we're going to kick him in the ass; twist his balls and kick the living shit out of him all the time. Our plan of operation is to advance and keep on advancing. We're going to go through the enemy like shit through a tinhorn.

There will be some complaints that we're pushing our people too hard. I don't give a damn about such complaints. I believe that an ounce of sweat will save a gallon of blood. The harder we push, the more Germans we kill. The more Germans we kill, the fewer of our men will be killed. Pushing harder means fewer casualties.

I want you all to remember that. My men don't surrender. I don't want to hear of any soldier under my command being captured unless he is hit. Even if you are hit, you can still fight. That's not just bullshit either. I want men like the lieutenant in Libya who, with a Luger against his chest, swept aside the gun with his hand, jerked his helmet off with the other and busted the hell out of the Boche with the helmet. Then he picked up the gun and he killed another German. All this time the man had a bullet through his lung. That's a man for you!

Don't forget, you don't know I'm here at all. No word of that fact is to be mentioned in any letters. The world is not supposed to know what the hell they did with me. I'm not supposed to be commanding this army. I'm not even supposed to be in England. Let the first bastards to find out be the goddamned Germans. Some day, I want them to rise up on their piss-soaked hind legs and howl 'Ach! It's the goddamned Third Army and that son-of-a-bitch Patton again!'

Then there's one thing you men will be able to say when this war is over and you get back home. Thirty years from now when you're sitting by your fireside with your grandson on your knee and he asks, 'What did you do in the great World War Two?' You won't have to cough and say, 'Well, your granddaddy shoveled shit in Louisiana.' No sir, you can look him straight in the eye and say 'Son, your granddaddy rode with the great Third Army and a son-of-a-goddamned-bitch named George Patton!'

All right, you sons of bitches. You know how I feel. I'll be proud to lead you wonderful guys in battle anytime, anywhere. That's all.

"Through a Glass, Darkly"

By George S. Patton, 1922

Through the travail of the ages,
Midst the pomp and toil of war,
I have fought and strove and perished
Countless times upon this star.

In the form of many people
In all panoplies of time
Have I seen the luring vision
Of the Victory Maid, sublime.

I have battled for fresh mammoth,
I have warred for pastures new,
I have listened to the whispers
When the race trek instinct grew.

I have known the call to battle
In each changeless changing shape
From the high souled voice of conscience
To the beastly lust for rape.

I have sinned and I have suffered,
Played the hero and the knave;
Fought for belly, shame, or country,
And for each have found a grave.

I cannot name my battles
For the visions are not clear,
Yet, I see the twisted faces
And I feel the rending spear.

Perhaps I stabbed our Savior
In His sacred helpless side.
Yet, I've called His name in blessing
When in after times I died.

In the dimness of the shadows
Where we hairy heathens warred,
I can taste in thought the lifeblood;
We used teeth before the sword.

While in later clearer vision
I can sense the coppery sweat,
Feel the pikes grow wet and slippery
When our Phalanx, Cyrus met.

Hear the rattle of the harness
Where the Persian darts bounced clear,
See their chariots wheel in panic
From the Hoplite's leveled spear.

See the goal grow monthly longer,
Reaching for the walls of Tyre.
Hear the crash of tons of granite,
Smell the quenchless eastern fire.

Still more clearly as a Roman,
Can I see the Legion close,
As our third rank moved in forward
And the short sword found our foes.

Once again I feel the anguish
Of that blistering treeless plain
When the Parthian showered death bolts,
And our discipline was in vain.

I remember all the suffering
Of those arrows in my neck.
Yet, I stabbed a grinning savage
As I died upon my back.

Once again I smell the heat sparks
When my Flemish plate gave way
And the lance ripped through my entrails
As on Crecy's field I lay.

In the windless, blinding stillness
Of the glittering tropic sea
I can see the bubbles rising
Where we set the captives free.

Midst the spume of half a tempest
I have heard the bulwarks go
When the crashing, point blank round shot
Sent destruction to our foe.

I have fought with gun and cutlass
On the red and slippery deck
With all Hell aflame within me
And a rope around my neck.

And still later as a General
Have I galloped with Murat
When we laughed at death and numbers
Trusting in the Emperor's Star.

Till at last our star faded,
And we shouted to our doom
Where the sunken road of Ohein
Closed us in its quivering gloom.

So but now with Tanks a'clatter
Have I waddled on the foe
Belching death at twenty paces,
By the star shell's ghastly glow.

So as through a glass, and darkly
The age long strife I see
Where I fought in many guises,
Many names, but always me.

And I see not in my blindness
What the objects were I wrought,
But as God rules o'er our bickerings
It was through His will I fought.

So forever in the future,
Shall I battle as of yore,
Dying to be born a fighter,
But to die again, once more.

"A man must know his destiny . . . if he does not recognize it, then he is lost. By this I mean, once, twice, or at the very most, three times, fate will reach out and tap a man on the shoulder . . . if he has the imagination, he will turn around and fate will point out to him what fork in the road he should take, if he has the guts, he will take it."

—George S. Patton, Jr.

Acknowledgments

Since my first book report in elementary school I've admired the U.S. military and how it has shaped the American identity. In the same spirit, recording these cherished moments and heroic events like Homer's chronicling of the Iliad or Virgil the Aeneid, shape our grand narrative.

World War II defined our nation. When our boys hit the beaches of Normandy, they were our boys. They were young and eager to serve their country. The enigmatic General Patton was the father figure to these boys. He taught them to be men, and set out to secure America's destiny.

To that ongoing achievement, I thank those who fought to provide the freedoms we enjoy today. Also, the children and grandchildren of those "boys" who maintain their memories or served themselves. I hope my work in a small way will contribute to their effort.

My thanks also go out to my publishers at Humanix, including Chris Ruddy, Mary Glenn, and Keith Pfeffer, for partnering with me on such an honorable subject. I am grateful to Victor Davis Hanson for his ongoing work to preserve the memory of our grand narrative.

Of course, thank you to David Treene and Brian MacDonald for their support on the Silence Patton project, and to those who have helped assemble content, and polish later rewrites, including

Erin Rodewald, Ila Stanger, and Ben Allison, all of whom helped me achieve my mission.

Finally and most certainly, to my greatest lieutenant, Margo.

Index

About the Author

Robert Orlando, BFA, School of Visual Arts, is a filmmaker, author, entrepreneur, and scholar. As an entrepreneur, he founded Nexus Media. As a scholar, his studies include film, religion, ancient and modern history and biography. As an award-winning writer/director, his films include the thought-provoking documentaries *Silence Patton*, *The Divine Plan*, and *Citizen Trump*. His books include *Apostle Paul: A Polite Bribe* and *The Divine Plan*. His work has been published in *Writing Short Scripts*, *American Thinker*, *The Catholic Thing*, *Daily Caller*, *HuffPost*, *Patheos*, and *Merion West*.

More Titles From Humanix Books You May Be Interested In:

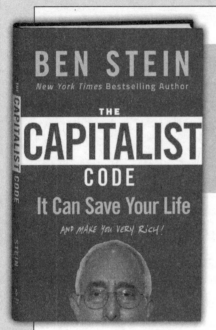

Warren Buffett says:
"My friend, Ben Stein, has written a short book that tells you everything you need to know about investing (and in words you can understand). Follow Ben's advice and you will do far better than almost all investors (and I include pension funds, universities and the super-rich) who pay high fees to advisors."

In his entertaining and informative style that has captivated generations, beloved *New York Times* bestselling author, actor, and financial expert Ben Stein sets the record straight about capitalism in the United States — it is not the "rigged system" young people are led to believe.

Scott Carpenter, Astronaut, NASA's Mercury Project says:
"By following the advice in The Simple Heart Cure, you can surmount the biggest challenge of all and win your battle against heart disease."

Heart disease kills more people than any other medical condition. In *The Simple Heart Cure*, you'll find this top doc's groundbreaking approach to preventing and reversing heart disease — an approach honed by his study of foreign cultures free of heart disease and decades of experience helping patients achieve a healthier heart at any age.

Mike Huckabee says:
"One of the most intellectually compelling and rational defenses of Christianity's role in America."

In *Dark Agenda: The War to Destroy Christian America*, David Horowitz examines how our elites — increasingly secular and atheist — are pushing a radical agenda. A *New York Times* bestselling author and leading conservative thinker, Horowitz warns that the rising attacks on Christians and their beliefs threaten all Americans — including Jews like himself.

"Most compelling defense of Christianity."
— *Gov. Mike Huckabee*

DARK AGENDA

The War to Destroy Christian America

DAVID HOROWITZ

THE WAR ON CA$H

How Banks and a Power-Hungry Government Want to Confiscate Your Cash, Steal Your Liberty and Track Every Dollar You Spend
And How to Fight Back

DAVID McREE

Newsmax Media says:
"The War on Cash is a must read for ALL Americans!"

The War on Cash is a wake-up call to everyone about the tactics being used by governments to restrict the public's use of cash and to abuse the laws for its own purposes. Powerful forces around the world are threatening your financial freedom. *The War on Cash* is a shocking look into the banks and power-hungry government plans to confiscate your cash, steal your liberty, and track every dollar you spend and how to fight back!

Get these books at Amazon and bookstores everywhere or checkout the FREE OFFERS! See:

HumanixBooks.com/Free